ETSY BUSINESS

Beginners Guide to Starting Your Own Etsy Business

&

Learn Etsy Marketing & SEO

SIMPLE STEPS TO MAXIMIZE PROFIT SELLING ON ETSY

TABLE OF CONTENTS

CHAPTER ONE: FUNDAMENTALS OF ETSY. 1
    ETSY FUNDAMENTAL HISTORY AND BASIC KNOWLEDGE 2
    ETSY VALUE SCHEME AND COMMERCE MODEL 3
    STARTING OPERATIONS 4

CHAPTER TWO: DOMINANT NICHES ON THE SITE AND HOW TO FIND THEM. ... 7

CHAPTER THREE: FINDING YOUR NICHE, YOUR BRAND, YOUR DESCRIPTION, YOUR ETSY IDENTITY. 15

CHAPTER FOUR: COMMON STARTING MISTAKES AND HOW TO AVOID THEM. 23

CHAPTER FIVE: ETSY SEO AND HOW TO USE IT. 31

CHAPTER SIX: USING SEO AND KEYWORDS PROPERLY IN YOUR TITLE AND DESCRIPTION TO RANK AT THE TOP. 41

CHAPTER SEVEN: HIDDEN FEATURES OF ETSY CAN PROVIDE YOU THE MOST POWERFUL BOOST IN SEARCH ENGINE RANKINGS. 49

CHAPTER EIGHT: BEST WAY TO PRICE YOUR PRODUCTS 57

CHAPTER NINE: HOW TO STAY ORGANIZED 65

CHAPTER TEN: MARKETING YOUR ETSY STORE. 71
    STEPS TO FOLLOW IN YOUR ETSY SHOP MARKETING 74

CHAPTER 11: POWERFUL BRANDING TECHNIQUES AND TACTICS. 93

CHAPTER 12: USING SOCIAL MEDIA AS A WAY TO PROMOTE YOUR ETSY STORE AND GENERATE CUSTOMERS. 111
    SOCIAL MEDIA OPTIMIZATION 116
    SOCIAL MEDIA MARKETING (SMM). 119
    ETSY AND THE MEDIA 120

CHAPTER 13: FACEBOOK, INSTAGRAM, PINTEREST. 123
    ETSY AND FACEBOOK 123
    INSTAGRAM AND ETSY 126
    ETSY AND PINTEREST 129

CHAPTER 14: SCALING UP, GOING PRO, AND GROWING YOUR ETSY EMPIRE.133

CHAPTER 15: WHY MOST SHOPS FAIL, AND HOW TO AVOID THAT................ 135

CHAPTER ONE:

Fundamentals of Etsy.

Before we begin to dive deep into the whole Etsy thing and begin to lose ourselves in conversations of unknown and unfamiliar territories, I will briefly give you an insight into what we are talking about when we say "e-commerce". Electronic commerce or e-commerce (sometimes written as eCommerce) is a business model that enables businesses and individuals to buy and sell online products. E-commerce operates in all four major business segments, including:

- Business to Business
- Consumer to Business
- Consumer to Consumer
- Business to Consumer

E-commerce, which can be performed on laptops, tablets, or smartphones, may be viewed as a digital equivalent of mail-order shopping catalogs. Through e-commerce transactions, almost every imaginable product and service is available, including books, music, plane tickets, and financial services such as stock investment and online banking. As such, the technology is considered to be very disruptive. E-commerce has helped companies establish a broader market presence by providing cheaper and more efficient channels of distribution for their products or services. The mass retailer Target, for example, has supplemented its brick-and-mortar presence with an online store that allows customers to buy everything from clothes to coffee makers to toothpaste to action figures. In comparison, Amazon was expanding the business with an online sales and product distribution platform focused on e-commerce. Not to be outdone, individual sellers have increasingly engaged through their websites in e-commerce transactions. Lastly, digital marketplaces like eBay or Etsy act as markets where multitudes of buyers and sellers come together to run businesses.

Now, going ahead to talk about what this section holds for you. The concept of this community is beyond imagination. It has kept on growing over time to become a system and model that works efficiently.

What does Etsy itself stand for? It's a secret known only to its founders and the company as making a point of throwing wildly made-up suggestions at the wonderers. This may be the acronym for "Easy to Sell Yourself", or the name of a guy who made delicious gelato while co-founder Rob was backpacking across Italy, as suggested by the company over the years (lightheartedly).

When it comes to Etsy, you are talking about one of the biggest e-commerce community ever created. Yes, I call it a community because it is more than just a market. It is an e-commerce society that went public on the 16th of April, 2015 and has been soaring since then delivering on super customer service and user comfort. From reliable sources of facts, in the year 2018, a gain of 165% in shares of Etsy was made this only just proves how efficient the system works. More history about this amazing community will be dished out.

Etsy Fundamental History and Basic Knowledge

Founded June 18th in the year 2005, by Robert Kalin, Haim Schoppik, Jared Tarbell and Chris Maguire, with its headquarters at Brokenly, New York, the USA with over 25 Million users, this is an eCommerce consumer market that allows artists to sell unique, handmade items to potential buyers worldwide. Etsy business model can be described as rather similar to Amazon or eBay but with the difference that Etsy offers both buyers and sellers an incredible value. On one hand, Etsy lets vendors sell their handmade crafts and make a living and on the other hand, it helps customers own special types of items and products based on the fact that they are usually crafted and handmade. That reality has contributed to Etsy's tremendous success. It began in 2005 as a simple website and is now mentioned as a public corporation with over $360 million in total funding.

Unlike Amazon and eBay, which are focused on the horizontal model that sells almost everything on their website, Etsy has chosen a vertical cognitive function by selling only craft products in specific categories. In addition to insights into Etsy business model and revenue growth techniques, let's go over its consumer groups, value propositions, and some other fascinating details too.

In 2018, Etsy generated US$ 603.7 million in revenue and reported a net profit of US$ 41.25 million. The company generates revenue mainly from three streams: its platform revenue includes a charge of 5% of the final selling value that an Etsy seller charges for each completed transaction, plus a listing charge of 20 cents per item;

Etsy reported in November 2016 that it paid US$ 32.5 million to consider buying Blackbird Technologies, a technology company that developed AI software that was used for shopping context/search apps.

Etsy can be seen as a basic marketplace model focused e-commerce platform that sells products and receives commission revenue. Even after getting a clear business model, Etsy has some basic operational functions in it. Etsy lists only exclusive items in the categories of art & craft, handmade and antique; Antique items can only be identified if they are twenty years old. Sellers can have a shop built. Etsy provides shipping worldwide, each retailer has feedback that helps buyers make the purchase decision, buyers have different payment options selected by the seller, and Etsy is more popular with women. It has a membership of 67 percent women.

Etsy value scheme and commerce model

Sellers

Creating a shop on Etsy is free; however, it costs $0.20 for each listing listed in the store. Every listing will live for 4 months on the shop's website, or until anyone buys the product. The shop owner sets the prices of the items, but Etsy reports 5 percent of each listing's final sale price. At the end of each month shop owners are sent a bill outlining the fees paid by Etsy, and they have to pay the fees until the 15th of the following month. Sellers can select, among others, through payment choices to sell to customers, including credit cards, debit cards, and PayPal. Etsy allows artists to showcase their items in front of the world. Sellers can create and name a shop on Etsy, as they wish. They have the option of adding as many items as they want to your shop. Sellers can select the selling price of their products as they see fit. Sellers can attach tags to their goods allowing easy identification of their products.

Buyers

Etsy helps customers to browse artists across the globe through the exclusive handmade items. Buyers are also permitted to buy antique products, and they can also get a product that has international shipping options shipped to their country. Besides, buyers can select from a list of categories by clicking on the link "Categories" under "More Ways to Shop" This will bring the user to a page of more than 30 categories, each of which has subcategories.

When a buyer views a product, they can decide to display each seller's positive percentage reviews to determine the shop's reliability. When a customer discovers a product they want to purchase, then click on "Add to Cart" and add the product to their "Shopping Cart" virtual Then the buyer can either continue shopping or purchase the item selected. Buyers do not have to have an account with Etsy to buy products and can register with a Facebook or Google account instead. Etsy has attracted criticism for consumer data management and privacy. According to the section on the website "Privacy Policy": "By using Etsy, you authorize Etsy to use your information in the U.S., Ireland and any other country where Etsy operates."

Going further to discuss how the system itself works and ensures to make sure customer satisfaction on both ends are satisfied.

- Sellers can sign in and list products for sale on the website, but then, It Isn't free to list items on Etsy. Etsy charges a fee to list any item that's valid for four months.
- Buyers can search these things, and order the things they want. Buyers will scan for the items using Etsy's advanced filters. Buyers must have the option to ask a question to the seller or can simply add the item to their cart.
- Buyers do a platform transaction. All purchases are made through Etsy. Etsy pays a 3.5 percent fee on a profitable transaction and transfers the remaining amount to the bank account of the seller.
- Buyers are given the option to rate and test products. These reviews are of assistance to other buyers interested in that product. The ranking system lets other customers discover whether the commodity is successful or not.

Starting operations

Etsy is popular as a side-business, as well as a place to buy products made from recycled and upcycled components, together with less expensive or more unusual versions of mass-produced items. Many of the items for sale are unique as part of their appeal to some shoppers. Product photos on Etsy appear to be either editorial or artistic rather than commercial style catalogs. Sellers may add tags to their products to help buyers find them, and buyers can search for locally available items. Etsy staff publish the list of items featured.

Most sellers are women in their twenties and thirties, who tend to be college-educated. Individual Etsy sellers decide which payment options to offer buyers; such options may include credit card, check, money order, PayPal, bank transfer, and Etsy gift card.

Etsy sellers range from hobbyists to professional artists who make a living with the site. Scaling up the production of handmade items may require more than full-time work, especially during the holiday shopping season, according to artists who developed their Etsy stores into their primary jobs.

Etsy headquarters are in Dumbo, Brooklyn, and it hosted open craft classes in the "Etsy Labs" Technology, customer service, marketing, PR, business, and communications teams on the site are working outside this office. Etsy Labs has a workspace providing equipment and donated materials, where members gather to make items, take workshops, and teach and attend special events. Etsy has a Berlin office too. Etsy announced that it was taking steps to hire more female engineers to improve its team's gender balance, as a website with a majority of female users but few female engineers. Thirty percent of Etsy engineers identified as "women or non-binaries" in 2019, and more than 30 percent were colored.

Etsy was one of the main members of Handmade Consortium, an effort in 2007 to encourage the purchase of handmade holiday gifts. Etsy has partnered with the West Elm retail chain to sell some Etsy products in their stores.

Talking about operation processes and all, let us quickly look into some of the basic reasons why Etsy has been such a successful eCommerce website.

Etsy provides a fascinating look at a company that found traction among a very passionate and idealistic group of people, rode that wave to massive growth and an IPO, and must now find growth through decisions often at odds with its earliest members' beliefs. In this growth study, we look at how they did it in the early days, their business decisions and dynamics that allowed them to scale up, and the company's efforts to continue to find the new lever for growth. The challenge for Etsy, now a $2 billion valued public company, is to find the growth public markets demand while at the same time doing their best to hold on to users who made them successful in the first place. Etsy has fostered a whole community of over 150 third-party applications and tools for empowering and helping sellers. Ety's community forums in the early days not only served as a place for sellers to get tips on how to improve sales, but they also acted as recruiting boards for new sellers and discussion hubs around the ideals of feminist craftsmanship. As Ungari puts it, "Etsy's incredible organic channel is his sellers' entrepreneurial push." It would be more appropriate to say that Ety's incredible organic channels are their sellers' anti-capitalist drive—at least quite early on. For the future, Etsy will continue to focus on non-transactional sales and exploit power sellers to attract new customers and retain loyalty to existing users. As with the April 2014 launch of Etsy Wholesale (in beta since April 2013), and the October 2014 release of Etsy's card reader, the company is likely to continue expanding their Seller Services. Etsy's card reader works in conjunction with the *Sell on Etsy* app (available on Android and iOS) by posting funds directly to shop payment accounts for sellers, synchronizing in real-time with online inventory, and emailing receipts that link back to the Etsy shop for feedback from the sellers. Also, the Etsy card reader allows "Quick Sales" for times when sellers might want to offer bundles or custom listings, such as at trade shows. Although the company is currently out of card readers, it was initially offered to any seller using Direct Checkout — a payment method that allows buyers to accept credit, debit, and Etsy gift cards and receive funds directly from these sales into their bank accounts in their currencies. The typical 3.5 percent transaction fee is waived for payments received through the Etsy Card reader. Rather, Etsy charges 2.75 percent, which is also what cost Square charges.

CHAPTER TWO:

Dominant Niches on the site and how to find them.

Once you understand that a niche is a very important factor in ensuring that you make not just sales but great sales on Etsy, then you are on your way to flourishing as a seller. You probably have no idea what I am talking about, no problem that is exactly why we are here. And if you already do, but you still need an insight into it or inspiration into how you can do better, then trust me, you have not come to the wrong place. Going further to discuss this section, we will be looking into what a niche is, how you can find them, the types, how they work, and many other niche-oriented factors.

Firstly, what is a Niche?

Niche means a distinct market segment, generally a targetable part of a market where customer demand is still unfulfilled. One example of successfully finding a niche on the market is to sell a product for sale in a geographic area where it was previously unavailable. Establishing a niche market business allows you to tap into an overlooked, or underserved customer base. It also turns out to be very effective because it is based on a small community addressing particular needs. When you open an eCommerce venture, your success will rely on finding the right niche to fill in on the market. There is no point in merely selling something that consumers already have or can buy at the same price as their product; much like competition on the high street, the company can only become a true success if you sell something different and better than ever.

In some cases, entering a niche market may also be a jumping-off point for a larger market to access. If you see success within a narrow niche, you can start adding additional products or services that are supplementary. Since you already have an existing client base, when you start from scratch these new areas will expand even faster than they should.

Throughout the e-commerce world, a niche is characterized as a particular market segment where high demand and low supply are present. Pronounced as either niche or "needs" (depending on if you want to sound fancy), a niche is simply a small, specialized market. Do you meet people who have dog pictures on all their clothes, pillows, and blankets? Those dog-printed items are a perfect example of a niche market — just like home-made jewelry, a particular sports team apparel, and early adopter tech gadgets. The niche markets are just more concentrated. The more the target group of consumers can be narrowed down, the more focused you are. A nationwide food-store chain is less specialized than a chain selling only organic products. A chain that only sells gluten-free, organic vegan food is more niche than a chain that only sells organic food. The further that the demand is regional, the greater the niche. Niche stores have fewer customers than department-style big stores, but that's exactly the point. With fewer customers, you can optimize your sales strategies more precisely, especially when your customers have much in common.

The question now is, why is it so important?

The short answer to that question is competition. There are many eCommerce stores online today, and if you're a small or medium-sized enterprise you don't have the resources to fend off rivals for every single market group. Choosing a particular customer segment (an eCommerce niche) and spending your money there is a better and more resourceful alternative. If you succeed, you can expand later on into other niches and build your brand market by market. Besides, niche customers tend to shop in similar patterns, making predicting and planning which products to sell and how to market them easier. Throughout your entire business, that trickles down, even reducing storage fees by reducing inventory hard to sell.

In general, the more you understand your shoppers, the more your sales strategies can be optimized. Pricing, deals (when and what kind), and sales techniques such as up-selling can all be tailored to specific types of the shopper to boost success.

Then customer outreach is there. Look at Amazon's Twitter account, which targets a wide, unspecified group of individuals. Their content is a lot of generic, feel-good content that is appealing to everyone, but also not to anyone. They're all over the place.

Listening to successful entrepreneurs, one ingredient of their success continues to return: Focus. This may sound universal, but the niche theory works just like focus, now let us see more reasons why you should set up your niche.

Stand out-You are unique and are more likely to be recognized by getting a niche. Without a niche, people would probably forget about you and your company. This can be applied to any undertaking based on products or services. Think of items you love, including Bose Speakers, which are known for their sound and audio quality of expectation. Or any market-oriented company specializing in business. Hertz car rental, for example, specializes in renting cars.

Your Ideal client-A key part of having a niche is having an ideal client. You can talk directly to your ideal client by getting a niche. This communication is important to help you attract individuals into your business. Not only are you not standing out without a niche, but you also are not talking to an ideal client or customer. "When you talk to everybody, you don't talk to anyone"

Specialize in a specific field – You have a specialty market by creating a niche that you can cater for in your products and services. You may know similar companies or competitors. When you are working on the first two components that have already been discussed above stand out and find the perfect customer. Your specific selling points will already be expressed in your brand statement and overall mission values. The niche and specialty you have are critical because you want your services to attract the right type of customers. That goes to your ideal customer. Your niche, however, will help you remember too. It can help capitalize on your unique skills, credibility, knowledge, and you as a brand if your niche is specialized. Especially if you're the corporate face.

Now let us talk about the dominant niches on Etsy. When I say dominant here, I mean niches that are heavily selling and hitting the top sales records. How then do you recognize dominant niches and how do you find them? Below are some niches that you should watch out for:

You can find online classes, eBooks, coaching, videos, and more offering self-improvement therapy and preparation. It is a dominant market that can be used on Etsy as a sales platform. Do you have experience overcoming doubts or changing aspects of your own or others' lives? That may include increased confidence, self-esteem, or assertiveness. Then think about tapping into this $10-billion market a year. Starting from this it could prove a lucrative and rewarding venture.

The beauty and cosmetics industry is rising at a rapid pace, offering a plethora of opportunities for beauty-savvy entrepreneurs to start their own online beauty company such as anti-aging clinics, online makeup tutorials, and beauty product eCommerce stores, to name only a few.

This market branch is also a very busy point and could be used to create a lot of traffic to boost Etsy sales. Many people would like this if they thrive in a particular area but do not know how to capitalize or market that talent. With this advice they could make use of that talent and now know how and where to do it. If you're a DIY expert or home decor enthusiast, you could capitalize on your expertise by offering online videos, eBooks, forums, and more with DIY and home decor advice and support online.

Anyone who loves children sells baby goods or provides online baby-focused services, such as help with planning baby showers or offering baby-related advice, maybe one of the most lucrative online niche markets to participate in or find themselves as a seller.

You'd agree with me that a lot of stickler people are waiting to eat, a massive online community is waiting to hear your tips, recipes, and culinary advice. Tap the huge online cooking niche by starting your cooking niche, writing a cooking blog or sharing your recipes, cooking items or materials online

If you're finding yourself a wine, beer, spirit, or some kind of alcohol connoisseur, participating in affiliate marketing programs for wine and beer clubs or online stores can be a fun and enjoyable way to share your awareness of your favorite tipple with other people. You might use this as a niche on Etsy as well, nothing drives the traffic during festival times like wines and beers following this and making a profit in that process.

If you are a sports lover with experience in a specific sport or many, you could use sporting activity resources and equipment as your niche on Etsy, you could also share your passion and knowledge of the sport with others in this lucrative online niche through the likes of photos, eBooks, selling sports apparel and more.

As for entertainment, we absolutely cannot get enough! Every year, with billions of dollars spent on entertainment, building your niche around this subject, such as reviewing movies and video games, is likely to be a lucrative undertaking.

Now talking about the Pros and Cons of Niches online. Some of you might not know, but as fun, as it sounds, there sides to it where you would have to pull through. Of course, we will talk about the advantages and merits, but then let us also look at potholes you should watch out for while on the journey of becoming the seller you have always envisioned yourself to be. Let us address both sides of the coin so that you will know what you are up against and how to deal with the reverse sides.

The basic merits of running a solidly planned niche according to the tips we have given above are stated below. You will observe that the first thing it knocks out is competition, that is because as we have stated earlier, that is the first most important reason why you are making a niche for yourself on Etsy. You should understand that the market can be very competitive and you might have to pull through with amazing ideas and come out different and distinct. Let us proceed.

Fewer competition

Since you are targeting a larger, massive market, there are chances that there will be more and serious competition. Connecting to the target market is often much easier when you're working in a specific niche. It cancels out the bidding for customers. Once clients visiting the websites hit their keywords which you have already registered under your shop or niche, it brings them directly to your profile, this way, you prevent them from wandering about looking for other things they might not even need. Simply put, your niche brings your customer directly to you.

Small budget

You will get more bounce to the ounce with niche use on Etsy, and save big on your marketing plans. Don't waste all of your time sending out flyers and brochures to all but focus on your target market instead. Even for small companies, the cost per conversion is substantially lower. Having a niche gives you comfort with reaching out to as many as possible without having to go through the conventional ways of marketing your shop which can be quite expensive if you would sit down to make estimations. You would probably not have to spend a dime once you begin to work with the very right niche for your shop.

Loyal clientele

The consumer is sovereign and if they're satisfied then they're no longer concerned. When consumers enjoy the goods or services and believe it fulfills their needs, then certainly they will come back for more. It's also likely that your audience will expand through their networks through word-of-mouth referrals and your brand's recommendations. Once your niche draws your customer to you, and you deliver on a good product, you own them already. This is because now they feel you are easy to find and your products are good. What beats that?

Now let us discuss the potholes I talked about earlier.

Low growth potential

It is debatable because when you're # 1 in your niche, only a small portion of the market can purchase your product, and thus the profit margin may not be as high as you expected. When you do not expand based on customer needs, there will be obstacles to your products/services and development. Once you create a niche for yourself, this means you have defined what your product and market is. That Is like saying you do just one thing out of a billion. This is the definition of limitation.

Tackling the big shots

The major runners on Etsy should start to feel uncomfortable after you have developed your niche and started to make a good profit. Etsy will sometimes also integrate your niche goods into their services as soon as they do so. Getting this done, brace yourself for some tough competition from the big players.

In conclusion, giving a summary of all that has been said earlier. You need to understand that having a functional well-strategized Niche is a key factor when you plan to make successful sales story on Etsy. The method of focusing all your marketing efforts on a limited, well-defined segment of your target audience is niche marketing. The idea of niche marketing is worth keeping in the back of your mind. It is worth noting also that there is a significant difference between seeking a marketing niche and niche. It's not niche marketing to sell your company to your niche. The selection of niches can make or break your eCommerce business. When deciding how to find a niche, you should look for niche markets that meet 3 different criteria. Now, to find a lucrative niche market, it's not mandatory to meet these 3 parameters, but it will yield the most reliable results from my personal experience.

- Net revenue
- Low Customer Service needed
- Large margins to income

A bad niche:

- No sales, or many distressed sales
- It needs a lot of customer service
- Small margins to benefit

Price point

The product's price will go a long way toward deciding whether the target audience is getting to your product.

Target market

Next, you should pick up niches with eCommerce markets that cater to upper-middle-class families and men. That's because goods that cater to 'discount' niche markets appear to demand a lot more consumer engagement while yielding a fair share of complaints and returns. On the other hand, goods that cater to affluent consumers will offer your clients who expect to obtain lots of individual attention, which will result in more work for you.

Lastly, you need to weigh several factors before you identify your niche market, and research the niche very carefully. The X-factor product(s) could take you weeks, months, or even years to find out.

But once you've worked it out, both of you are set to enter the real world. Once you have built your niche product, you have to put your marketing cap on it and brand yourself.

You need to consider many variables, such as geographic position, various types of customers, age group, gender, or unique needs, before making a list. Targeted brides, for example, are too wide of a variety – a niche market would target beach wedding dresses or handmade bridal veils for the artsy bride. Once you've built the list of people who are going to be your future clients, you need to do some homework on them too. You can start by conversing with one of your potential clients. Figure out just what he/she is looking for, and come up with a panacea for their individual needs.

Figure out your future customers' tastes for the drug. It is an important aspect you should be paying attention to. Please operate from the viewpoint of the Customer. The problem is what are they going to want? Do they want high quality or low quality? Target low or reasonable? What kind of features are they looking for? Was insurance a big factor? color schemes they would prefer? When it comes to these interests, you will be able to communicate with your clientele. Research the market, and win loyal customers. Seek to find out more about your potential buyers, manufacturing costs, marketing costs, and, most importantly, the products of your rival before you bring your product onto the market. This will help us recognize the customers that will not concentrate the marketing efforts on. This will save you time and money through marketing campaigns and advertising. Simple things like talking with your potential buyer, flipping through shops and magazines specific to your niche, and even searching for your product on Google will help you understand your company's prospective audience. You will quickly find your target demographic if you want to sell homemade bath products – people with allergies, people with a big love for homemade products, vegans, etc. Word of - mouth and marketing on the internet will help you expand and win loyal clients.

The importance of your niche cannot be overemphasized. It is important. As we move on, we will keep talking about all these basic factors that will help you become the business person you have always wanted to be on Etsy. Going further, keep an open mind to the ideas that will be delivered and given as they are of high quality and have been strategically arranged to help you achieve the kind of business presence you have always needed for your shop outlet on Etsy.

CHAPTER THREE:

Finding your Niche, your brand, your description, your Etsy identity.

Concentrating on finding your Etsy niche, as it is as important as your market and product itself. Now, before you go ahead to find the niche that perfectly fits into what you have in mind, there are basic factors you should look into and understand.

The Etsy platform has made it easier for craftspeople to take advantage of their talent. But to be a good Etsy seller, you'll need to do more than just set up your shop. If you want to stand out from your rivals, you need to practice the entrepreneurial skills that all small business owners will know. But again, with over two million active total sellers as of 2019, Etsy has never been more crowded. Whatever market you are in, you're likely to compete with hundreds of other successful sellers that offer similar products. To make Etsy a viable business option, the sellers need to stand out. Yet even with heavy competition for attention from buyers, you can improve your listings and cater to more consumers without adjusting your inventory or overhauling your whole strategy for sellers. You have to do it right to be able to stand out. Let us then outline the factors you should look for that will increase your effect on your presence, find your niche, and build your own identity.

Become a Member of the system. The Etsy group is huge and being part of it is in your best interest. Seek to engage in discussions on the web by giving input to other sellers and by reaching out for advice to your favorite Etsy sellers. Look for local activities in your neighborhood to engage in, to create in-person outreach. Opportunities to spread awareness and network with other sellers and potential customers are to attend activities within your own cultures, such as meetups and pop-up shops. You can reach out to self-knowledge and allow yourself to grow by finding out necessary information that could be enlightening.

Boost your Photo-shot game. Without images of professional quality, your goods won't entice people to click on any crowded marketplace like Etsy. Taking top-notch pictures means you'll possibly need to purchase, borrow, or rent professional-grade camera equipment to get the best results. Lighting is also key to a perfect picture — no matter how good your camera is. Consult a product images manual on how to light and shoot. There are a lot of printed picture guides and an array of free online material that will help you step up your product images. Should not be afraid to touch them up after you've taken your pictures. And if you can't afford the expensive picture tools, online or as applications, there are great free alternatives. Although you never want to distort your pieces, it makes a big difference to make sure your colors are true to life, or to crop images for a clearer view of the product. A photo worth a thousand words, and more on Etsy. Make sure you are using standard, high-resolution images that properly view your items. Using through angles and depths to give information about your pieces. Posting several pictures is also a smart idea, with at least one of those photos showing the product in practice. While you don't need to employ a skilled photographer, you need to use a decent camera to highlight your items in a good light.

Research customer view — and avoid their errors. Take the time to browse through Etsy, as if you were a customer. Check in the niches you want to conquer, and test your rivals.

You can ask questions like:

- What do I love about the things I'm most drawn to in my niche or the top sellers?
- How does this seller do in their images and details that I am not doing well?
- How do the commenters think about the shop/service/items of the seller?
- Who drives me away from a seller I don't like buying from?
- How does this seller do to throw me off in their pictures and details, and am I doing any of those things?
- What do the commenters think about the shop/service/items of the seller?

Do not steal outright what other sellers do, but be mindful of what works in your room and change your products accordingly; no one has a monopoly on being up-to-date on what works in your niche. Analyze what your rivals are doing every six months, or so; trends and popularity on platforms like Etsy can shift rapidly.

Optimize SEO Titles. Etsy is at its heart a search engine. Your titles are one of the key ways in which it determines how to index things, and having your title right can help your items appear in a search faster — that is, make sure that your titles follow best practices in search engine optimization (SEO). Below are the keys to the optimization of the product titles:

Stay down-to-earth. Include your product's fabric or other material names, height, or other identifying features that will come up when someone tries to find what you are selling.

Different words are used for the same object. For example, if you sell key chains, the title of your leather embossed key chain may be "Personalized key fob leather key ring leather embossed keyholder"

Bear in mind that it's not just the title of the item that brings people in. The primary purpose of the title should be to get the goods to appear in a quest. Great images, explanations of the goods, and other elements are what will get customers to buy. Most of the future clients would come from searches over the Internet. Making your Etsy store SEO-optimized is critical. Doing so can help rate your shop and items in web searches near the top. Be sure to remember everything from your company name to the names and specifications of the products. While writing product descriptions, any aspect of the product (size, color, condition, uses, shipping, etc.) should be discussed to reduce any consumer complaints while satisfying the search engines. Besides, keeping the shop updated and adding new content can also help refine the search results for others.

Show off stories. Yeah, taking professional-looking photographs is necessary, but putting it on a bland backdrop is not the only way to go and it isn't the best way to stand out. When you've got something to wear — shoes, bags, jewelry, belts, or other accessories, reveal them styled. When your item is for a particular reason, it should be seen in practice, not just in a "studio" environment. Show outdoors and in use, for example, a portable campfire or tent, or show a picture of someone walking their dog with the leash you sell. The goal with product images is not only to demonstrate exactly how your goods look but also to appeal to the shopper's imagination:

Could they see themselves with your items? Are they drawn in by the lifestyle which you sell? We would have been!

Keep your explanations short. Your explanations of your products are a major sales pitch for shoppers. Users reading your reviews have found, clicked on, and are searching for information to determine whether to buy or not. You're halfway to a sale and what you're doing about your company will make or break the sale. Shoppers want the specifics at this point in their journey, so tell them what they need to know to convince their purchase. Dimensions, delivery times, size details, material information, and all other data about your product can ensure that when you buy from your online store, consumers know exactly what they are getting. Do your pieces sound as good as possible, along with the facts and figures: Is your pottery hand-thrown? Dip-dyed Rugs in tiny lots? Is one concept of a kind? Whatever it is that should be at the forefront and core of the offerings. Try adding a custom quote on how fantastic your goods are as social proof to drive home the value you give customers.

Choose a username descriptive of your store. Only small items can make a difference in an environment as crowded as Etsy does. The user name must be unforgettable, as well as concise. Why? For what? Imagine browsing on Etsy for the prints. Who would you trust more, a seller whose username is "EastCoastPrintCo" or a "tea-wise" seller? Getting a username that reflects your professionalism shows that you are a serious seller capable of satisfying their order. This is also a space for selling deals and craftsmanship of your products. When a customer buys backpacks and sees "Canvas_Works_Virginia" as your username, they can be enticed to click on your shop and browse the totes and other products. Branding is not just about your shop and the items you make. It's for you too. Joining the Etsy community, making unique goods, offering outstanding service, and establishing yourself as an expert by blogging are all ways to set up your brand. Try designing your shop with a distinctive logo. Using your new logo, advertising, business cards, and packaging on your store. This will help create faith and trust with your customers and show the quality of your goods and brand.

Open a Blog. Even if your goods are exclusive, other sellers will likely offer similar pieces. What separates your items depends on how much you market your shop outside the Etsy web site. Starting a blog to share information about your goods is one way apart from Etsy, to improve exposure. Try sharing information about yourself and your goods (how they are made, etc.), and make sure to use the correct SEO keywords. Another great idea is to write about topics which concern your shoppers. For example, if you're selling environmentally friendly goods, write blog posts about how your shopper can be more environmentally friendly in their everyday lives.

Provide the best service to a customer. Shoppers are more likely to purchase products from stores where they get better service. Provide the choice of contacting customers via email, phone, or chat. Keep your customers satisfied by answering any questions and reviews promptly. Be sure to react kindly to your customers if there are any issues, even though you believe the issue wasn't your fault. When you're on social media, make sure to answer any questions or inquiries. Follow up with your customers during the buyer's journey to make sure they are enjoying their purchase. Sending out thank you emails or telling your customers about their shopping experience shows your commitment to offering outstanding service. Your best marketing efforts will come from pleased, satisfied customers who use word-of-mouth marketing tactics to recommend your goods to their mates.

Say a profile story. If a shopper moves over to your shop page from your product page, what will they see? This should be a highly curated room that tells a story about who you are and why your company is better than your rivals, and in your profile is one of the best places to do so. Shoppers reading your profile are searching for more information about you and want to see if your company is dependable. Or put it another way, your profile is a marketing tool.

Market Your Social Media Brand. Social media plays an important role in today's marketing campaigns and strategic networking approaches are a must to create a loyal following. To get going, at least create profiles on Facebook, Twitter, and Instagram for your shop, and other social media networks if you have time to handle them. You will build a friendship with your clients with social media. Interacting with followers is a common engagement source which shows how personable your brand is. Anything as easy as enjoying and reacting to comments let customers know that their support is appreciated. Such networks also act as a convenient source for influencers to discover the brand and share it on social media with their followers.

Let us proceed to discuss how your description also takes you a step forward to reaching where you want to be.

Now, the customer clicked on your profile and you used the right niche to do so, the customer is now on your website, looking for the perfect product so fits their needs. The very last move is to persuade the client to click on the "add to cart" button. How? How? With a proper description of the commodity. One of the most common errors made when writing product descriptions is that copywriters simply explain the goods instead of selling the items with the description to their target market, which means – one of the most critical aspects of your online shop when it comes to conversion is the product description. But then, because it holds tremendous strength, it can be difficult to write a good copy of the drug. Especially when you have a long list of things to work through on your product page it can be mind-numbing. A clear explanation of the product has the power to turn a casual shopper into a buyer which generates revenue. Yet so many online retailers are merely asking shoppers about the commodity instead of selling it.

Now, when we talk about the niche or product description, basic factors should be put into consideration, some questions should be asked let us see some of these questions.

- Who is this product for? What's their demographic? What are their interests? If you know this detail, the better suited you'll be to explain how your company gives them value and how you can interact with your audience.
- What are the specifics of the product and what sets the company apart? This includes the basic measurements, characteristics, and features of your company, as well as what makes you distinct from competitors.
- How will your customers use this product? Is it supposed to be used indoors or outdoors? Any special or funny place you can use this product?
- How do your customers use your product? Was it while they're traveling? Is it a seasonal item?
- How should anyone buy and use your product? Why does it make their lives better? Which question does it solve? Once, is there something special, fun, or funny?
- How does your product work? It isn't necessarily important, but if it's a new device or piece of technology, you might want to explain how it works to your audience to avoid any misunderstanding. And, you don't want to make this method sound like rocket science. Think: easy-peasy.

Discussing the subject matter further, lest we also look into some factors that should be considered important and how they can help you in product description and identity.

Focus on the Consumer Benefits

As a company owner, you are naturally eager to share all of the benefits of your goods. You want to prove that your product has the best features and most exclusive specs. The customer, however, is not generally interested in the bland features of the product. Instead, they want to learn how it will help them. A product function is a factual statement about the product that offers technical details. A product value, on the other hand, explains how the product will change the buyer's life.

Using Natural Language and Tone

When you read your summary aloud, would it sound like a real conversation that you might have with your friend? How does it sound like a computer-generated string of words? If your product description isn't something that you would say to your friend about the product, then it's time to inject a little life into them.

Bringing this natural tone – one that you would use in a real conversation – will help your customer connect with your brand. Your voice is one of the most effective ways of differentiating you from your competition. And, communicating with your particular audience is a perfect way.

Bridge the Gaps Between Features and Benefits

You're already aware that you should describe how your product works and why your customer should invest in it. To give your audience a little nudge, make sure that you spell out the benefits of your product within the product features description. In other words, explain "how" a certain feature is beneficial to their lives and "why" it's an essential purchase.

Eliminate Buyer's Guilt

The product should be presented as important, make it sound as though your product would save them money in the long-run, Highlight its multiple features.

Appeal to The Audience's Imagination.

Research has found that if consumers keep a product, it enhances their willingness to own the product. The dilemma is that as an e-commerce platform, you can't touch and feel. This means that you have to cater to your audience's imagination through words so that they can visualize what it would be like to touch, smell, and own your product.

Use Power Terms That Sell

There are some words and phrases that automatically evoke an emotional response in humans. Luckily for Shopify store owners, this also increases profits. By being mindful of these words and phrases, you can more quickly persuade your clients to take the plunge and make the purchase.

In conclusion, some of the most critical business decisions an e-commerce owner has to make are which niches to pursue. It involves not only choosing niches you're personally passionate about, but also lucrative niches whose market can sustain your business. You have to understand things like consumer demand, niche customer shopping preferences, and the quality of items. The secret to selling on Etsy is to be trustworthy. Focus your marketing strategies on customer satisfaction and how you'll show the business to the public. Keep up to date on developments and continue to try new tips through analysis. Through developing your company in every area (outreach, SEO, product quality), these activities will help develop your brand and credibility on a great marketplace. After you want to come forward with a product to sell. You will learn the art of using Keywords. Etsy listings are shown according to the Etsy search algorithm known as Etsy SEO. Make sure you make the best use of keywords in your listings. Include the keywords in various categories of product listings including the product title, the summary, and other sections of listing. You need to get the full insight into the Etsy SEO job, to get higher exposure to your store and thus gain shoppers. So far, you have come to know what is rolling on Etsy. How the top players are doing, what to offer on Etsy, and What sells best on Etsy? You can start from the very beginning and be sure to know that you will hit with consistency and innovation what you want to be a master of.

CHAPTER FOUR:

Common starting mistakes and how to avoid them.

Running a shop on Etsy is like climbing a mountain. Often you're on the up-and-up, and other times you encounter challenges that impede your progress. As a rock climber, you need the right equipment, experience, and determination to hit the top. This is exactly why you are here right now trying to get the insight you need into being the seller/business person you want to be. It takes time and preparation, and that's why it's important to plan yourself for success by avoiding common mistakes that other sellers make on their way to being what they aspire.

Running a company is full of inevitable challenges and obstacles, ones that are likely to test your endurance and resolve. Also, with the countless number of open and customizable eCommerce platforms available today, many things go wrong when developing, launching, or managing an online company. Whether you're just getting ready to open your first online store or are still running several stores, you're bound to experience a challenge that will hold your company back. With that said, there are ways you can prevent some of the more common mistakes faced by entrepreneurs.

It all differs from and to different levels, from selecting the wrong eCommerce platform to not understanding user experience, in this blog you'll learn what mistakes to avoid — and how to set yourself up for eCommerce success.

Each eCommerce seller knows that when it comes to selling goods online, content is king. If customers cannot hold a product in their hands, top-quality content can bridge the gap – through rich knowledge, pictures, images, and more. Optimizing web content helps producers and retailers alike; but still, we also see product listings that leave shoppers under-informed or simply uninspired.

Etsy marketing isn't an exact science, and that means there's a lot of trial and error on the road to creating a profitable online company. There are a variety of common errors that newcomers to online marketing make when it comes to promoting their online stores. Without being aware of these e-commerce marketing errors, it's easy to replicate them time and time again — a waste of money and a surefire way to lose the valuable business opportunities you need to expand. If you're serious about bringing your eCommerce venture to the next level, your company needs a strong path and emphasis on established eCommerce marketing strategies. Gone are those days when we need to reach the busy streets, bear with the heavy traffic only to be able to buy what we need in shops and supermarkets. Today, the way that people spend their money has changed drastically. They no longer spend time on car fuel just to be able to shop. Alternatively, the shopping is done at the touch of a button or pressing the "add to cart" option. And, hence the rise of online retailers, who often seek to offer the goods and services that customers most search for while trying to shop online.

Coming to an understanding that everyone one on this planet is a buyer and we need resources, every one of us needs! This is the consumer base of E-commerce! What you need to do is start selling what you got and allure your customers. But this isn't as easy as read! Some participate in the race to win. But the winner is the one who doesn't make mistakes and time-wasting errors when selling a product online. Yeah, there are many common yet important mistakes online sellers do when they sell a product online. With the power and ability of the digit-tech right now, Starting running an e-commerce company on Etsy has never been easier. But there are important things to keep in mind to keep your company afloat. Many online portals have shut shop due to their inability to keep pace with the changing times and needs. You must avoid the mistakes they make and play along with the dynamics of the online platform. Seize the day to stay ahead and keep clear of these mistakes. Let us look into some of these mistakes and how to avoid them. Embedded in this section is the secret to avoiding falling where others fell avoiding the stumbles that others failed to see. Let us proceed:

Etsy is one of the most secured and efficient platforms, that doesn't we do not recognize the efforts and presence of other platforms that are doing fine that being said,

Choosing the right eCommerce Platform: If you're just beginning your eCommerce company or you've been running an online store for some time, your eCommerce platform will make (or break) your company. Not only does your eCommerce platform decide how you present your goods and sell to consumers, but it also plays a part in how you draw users, and how you scale your business over time. The last thing you want is to choose a platform that restricts your business development, one that doesn't align with your current systems or provide the level of control and flexibility that you want. Choosing the wrong eCommerce platform can lead to a range of issues like revenue loss, lower conversions, traffic reduction, security issues, poor design, and much more. This critical mistake could mean having to invest even more time, money, and energy into updating your platform or migrating to a different one altogether.

Another mistake that can be made is not identifying and knowing your target market. You have goods, you have a business plan, and you have a website-what else do you need? Unfortunately, simply getting an offer and a place to sell it isn't enough to truly be successful with eCommerce (or any form of company, really). One of the biggest mistakes a business owner can make is not identifying their target market, and taking the time to learn what makes them tick.

When your shop or niche material is not CRO or SEO-friendly

If your eCommerce company relies on organic traffic to attract clients, then the content of your website should be written with both the customer and the SEO in mind. Many businesses make the mistake of afterthought handling their content — not realizing that each piece of content is an opportunity to draw more traffic and convert customers. From your Homepage to your product reviews, you need to deliver content that is on point for your target market, is designed for search engine traffic, and entices users to purchase your products. If you are working with an SEO firm or going the DIY path, investing in content that is SEO and CRO-friendly is worthwhile. This means using the right high-quality keywords for your market and creating copies that have been made for sale.

Neglecting to make the user experience a priority

Despite more e-commerce stores going live every day, consumers have countless shopping choices, making it harder to convince them to go shopping despite you. As many as 38% of customers leave a website that doesn't have an appealing interface and 46 percent of website visitors say that a "lack of message" will make them leave the page. That said, maximizing user experience will be at the core of the marketing plan for e-commerce. Simplicity, pleasing style, helpful photos, explanations, and SEO are going to go a long way here.

No Clear Brand Image or Identity

A commodity doesn't make a mark. Although Nike may be known for its sneakers, they've put in the effort to establish a powerful brand identity, logo, and message. The Nike "swoosh" is known all over the world, and its "Just Do It" tagline is plain, recognizable, and inspiring. Don't make the mistake of believing that the goods are perfect enough to sell themselves. To build a profitable business, you will need to develop a strong brand identity that is relatable to your audience and will be conducive to viral brand awareness. Be Authentic, Be Consistent When you've done your market research, you will have a good understanding of what your audience is looking for, and what sort of language appeals to them. So, it's only a matter of being clear and unwavering in the messaging. When your brand reflects high-quality, trustworthiness, fun, affordability, etc., then these values should be apparent in all of your content, branding, and marketing.

Overthinking it

In e-commerce, it's pretty easy to get lost, particularly if you don't prioritize. If you care too much about little things, you risk not seeing the forest for the woods. When you start, seek to remove all the things that bring little to no value to your company and concentrate on cost-effective approaches that will enable you to improve business performance instead.

Choosing the wrong CMS

That e-commerce marketing error is making the wrong option in e-commerce CMS platforms. It might be tempting to cut down costs by opting for a cheap partner, but this isn't the best way to cut corners if you want to provide your shoppers with an excellent shopping experience.

Poor Customer Service

Customer support covers several items. It involves how you respond to user messages via your website. It's how you react to questions and comments on social media. It's how you answer customers' concerns over the phone and by email. It's every contact you have with a customer that needs your attention and product. Weak customer service (including poor response time, showing impatience, not giving refunds, etc.) is the surest way to lose current customers and prevent attracting new ones.

Not honing your product details

Too many product pages are flat lists of features and technical information. Information is crucial for making informed buying decisions, but the way you choose to promote your products within your e-commerce store is equally essential for consistent sales growth. Reflect on the advantages that buyers will get from their purchase. Enhance the attributes that make your goods and services better than the ones offered by your rivals. Think about your potential consumers and their pain points, and use explanations to illustrate how each product can solve problems. Be There If They Need You. You should be open to your users and customers at every stage of your selling cycle — from obtaining details to checking out, to follow-up. It means that they don't have any problems, or if they do, you can fix them easily and effectively. If you take forever to respond, depend on automated responses, just give one-word answers, or have a "tough luck" attitude, you will build a long trail of dissatisfied customers. Your customers are the lifeblood of your firm. Not only is it easier to and more lucrative to retain a current client, but the possibility of them bringing more customers to you is enhanced when you provide excellent customer service.

Settling for low average value for the order

Settling for a low average order value you do know that the cost of having three customers to spend $50 each is much better than getting one customer who spends $150. You can also concentrate on increasing consumer loyalty and encouraging potential customers to make more purchases from your shop, instead of concentrating your approach solely on boosting your sales funnel.

Forget about maximizing the ads

E-commerce marketing should truly be at the heart of your business. It is time to let go of the idea that "good goods are selling themselves," and spend time creating a coherent plan for digital marketing. To consistently pull in customers, you'll need strategic SEO, high-quality, helpful content, and smart retargeting. Much less, and you'll fail to get the leads you're looking for and the conversions.

To discuss this further, let us address more mistakes that are avoidable.

Sticking to the basics

Today, rich content is the name of the eCommerce game. Rich and A+ content (interactive media, sell-sheets, video demos) empowers brands to offer compelling shopping experiences through digital touchpoints – while simple, meat-and-potatoes knowledge puts you at an immediate disadvantage.

Do not expect to make money by simply listing a commodity

Selling online takes more than advertising a product for sale on your website. Surprisingly, many people still assume that by publishing a product for sale ensures that the buyers will come. It may seem easy to throw a product up for sale, post it on social media, and expect your followers to purchase your item, but it takes a lot more effort than that. Instead, concentrate on cultivating the audience by adding value to their lives. You can do this by creating useful, free opt-ins, sharing other people's work on social media, and designing an online marketing strategy that makes sense for your company.

Lack of brand identity

With so many product listings to choose from, customers need to understand why your brand is different – and your passion will live on your product pages. Putting the company's story forward can be a good differentiator, demonstrating that you have a solid background and a reputation for quality. In eCommerce, linking to your website, social media accounts, and other tools can help put customers at ease, boost SEO, and even close the deal.

Not realizing who you're selling to

Creating a community is important for selling on Etsy because if you don't know how to help with what you know, you aren't able to build goods and services that better people's lives. First, you want to find out what it is that you bring and how you can support most with what you learn. There are several ways to narrow the scope but there are two ways to identify a target audience for simplicity: demographics and psychographics. Demographics include age, gender, income, level of employment, and level of education. Psycho graphics is a little different and lets you identify your target audience through personality, beliefs, interests, behaviors, and behavior. A combination of both demographic and psychographic characteristics will work well, or you can choose one. Instead, you are going to want to write down your ideal target audience something you can quickly relate to. It offers you a buffer when writing product copy, reviews, blog posts, and social media.

Getting through with one pic

Life is a 360-degree experience – but some online sellers think their customers would be satisfied with only one view. Check out top Amazon sellers – you'll see they also have multiple product pictures from a variety of angles. Since online shoppers cannot walk around your item in person, multiple photos provide the next best thing.

All-caps lettering

To mark yourself directly as an eCommerce beginner, use all-caps lettering. This is rough on shoppers' eyes and eventually becomes illegible in large amounts. Having names, subtitles, or advertisement copy set in all caps WILL MAKE THE READER FEEL LIKE YOU ARE YELLING AT THEM. (See?) Make your type natural and varied; using extreme tactics to catch people's attention will only drive them to another product or site.

Promoting more than adding value

Is there anything worse than someone who constantly talks about themselves? Eventually, we learn to tune out those people, because they aren't adding value to the conversation. The same goes for selling and sharing online. When all people do is share their product for sale without attempting to add value or educate their followers, they're not influencing them to buy. This type of strategy may turn off potential customers. Try flipping your strategy and sharing relevant, valuable, and helpful content with your target audience, then asking for the sale later. An 80 percent ratio of sharing content to 20 percent promoting and selling is a good rule of thumb.

Providing imprecise product images

To become sloppy when writing details of your product will definitely cost you money. Etsy was known to suspend online businesses and provide their customers with incorrect product descriptions. Do not forget when selling any form of product on Etsy that you have a lot of competition. If buyers realize that your product details are inaccurate, some words are misspelled, or incorrect adjectives are used, you risk the chance of receiving many complaints from the customers. Not to mention your irate customers negative feedback and rating. If in the course of time errors like these continue, Etsy may suspend your company. You need to plan to file an Etsy appeal so that you can get your company back to normal service.

CHAPTER FIVE:

Etsy SEO and how to use it.

First of all, to ensure that we are on the same page of this book, let us understand some basic terms that would be required for you to have a smooth ride in this section. Let us understand what the SEO means on its own before we go ahead to find out how it can be used.

Search Engine Optimization (SEO) is the method of growing the quality and quantity of website traffic by making a website or web page more accessible to online search engine users. The SEO applies to optimize unpaid outcomes (known as "normal" or "real" outcomes) and excludes direct traffic and pay placement purchases. Furthermore, it may target various types of searches, including image search, video search, academic search, news search, and vertical search engines unique to the industry. Another SEO strategy is to promote a platform to raise the number of backlinks, or links to the inbound. As an Internet marketing technique, SEO considers how search engines function, the computer-programmed algorithms dictating search engine behavior, what people are looking for, the actual search terms or keywords entered into search engines, and the search engines are favored by their target audience. SEO is done as a website will attract more traffic from a search engine when the search engine results page (SERP) ranks higher on the websites. Instead, these tourists will eventually become customers. SEO differs from local search engine optimization in that the latter focuses on improving the online presence of a company so that search engines can view its web pages when a user joins a local search for their products or services. Alternatively, the former concentrates mostly on regional or foreign searches.

In order to attract customers, under the umbrella of SEO, digital marketing which requires the use of the Web, mobile devices, social media, search engines, and other platforms also became necessary. Some marketing experts find digital marketing to be a radically new field needing a new approach to consumers and new ways of understanding how customers act in contrast with conventional marketing. Digital marketing aims and is open to a particular section of the consumer base. Digital marketing is on the rise and involves search engine advertising, email advertising, and sponsored tweets – anything that combines customer feedback marketing or a two-way business-customer interaction. Web marketing varies from Internet marketing. Internet marketing is an Internet-only advertisement, while digital marketing can be done via mobile devices, a subway network, a video game, or a smartphone app.

SEO (Search Engine Optimization) seeks to attract as much traffic as possible into a website by placing it at the top of the results of a search engine. Businesses and individuals use SEO to increase the exposure of their websites and content to improve traffic, and therefore business. Companies also employ SEO specialists to introduce these techniques to optimize organic traffic, which is the traffic that arrives at a website and not as a result of paid search activities, like pay-per-click (PPC). SEO is a form of digital marketing primarily focused on pushing a website higher in search results on sites like Google, Yahoo, and Bing. Search engines are the most popular vehicle to carry organic (non-paid) traffic to a website, making SEO highly competitive: A good strategy will bring high visibility to a company. Search engines will also see through an effort to appeal to the search engine rather than the customer and as a result, would rate the site lower. This technique, called cloaking, uses all the keywords and techniques required to make a website appear information-rich and useful on the surface to draw attention but does not give value to the user. The first search engines were fairly inefficient as they couldn't do anything more than look for sites with unique keywords in them. Search engines have developed over time, and are sophisticated enough in their search algorithms to use hundreds of variables.

Going further to discuss the subject matter,
- Usage of keywords or commonly used terms relating to the function of a web. When a user types a sentence into a search engine, the search engine combs through the pages containing that sentence.
- Consistent changes to the website. Websites that have not created new content in a while would be considered less important. Some broken links or similar defects will downplay the ranking of a site.

- The basic usability and functionality of a website need to be paid attention to. Search engines take into account the organizational structure and ease of use of the website, as well as the quality of information and content found within. In search results, simpler pages with a straightforward, descriptive, and useful language appear to rank higher.
- Find ways to provide connections to other websites (back links). A search engine considers this as an indicator that your website is important enough for others to access. The better the site that connects to you rated the higher.
- Do not show the name of your business or other significant marketing material as part of an image, as the text in an image would not be included in the indexed results of a search engine.

Now taking a quick peek into what and how SMO (Social Media Optimization) is all about SEO (Search Engine Optimization).

Social media optimization (SMO) is the use of social media networks to monitor and expand the message and web presence of a company. Social media optimization can be used as a digital marketing technique to raise awareness of new goods and services, interact with consumers, and enhance possible negative news.

Social media optimization (SMO) is the use of social media networks to monitor and expand the message and web presence of a company.

Social media optimization can be used as a digital marketing technique to raise awareness of new goods and services, interact with consumers, and enhance possible negative news.

Digital marketing can be found on various social media sites, including Facebook, Twitter, Instagram, Snapchat, YouTube, and Pinterest.

Search engine optimization (SEO) has been the norm for digital marketing initiatives for many years. Although social media optimization and search engine optimization have similar goals – to generate web traffic and increase awareness of a company's website – search engine optimization is the process of increasing the quality and quantity of website traffic by raising the visibility of a website or a web page for users of a web search engine, especially Google.

More recently, social media marketing has come to the fore, often converging with SEO and in some cases replacing it as the most powerful way to reinforce a brand, lead generation, increase the exposure of a business in the online space, and communicate with an audience. Digital marketing can be used on various social media sites, including Facebook, Twitter, Instagram, Snapchat, YouTube, and Pinterest.

Social media management also guides the public to the company's web site from these social media sites, where more information can be received. For example, a campaign to raise awareness on social media about a new car that guides the visitor to a company website that provides information about where local dealerships are located and how to schedule a test drive.

Companies that use multiple social media platforms can use Internet-based tools designed to improve organization and content delivery. These tools enable an employee who is tasked with creating social media content to simultaneously schedule content across multiple platforms, as well as respond to any posting commitments including comments or messages from the public.

Sharing tools on social media sites allow users to almost instantly exchange content over the Internet. Because of this, several companies are trying to build content that users pass on to their friends and contacts. This tactic, called viral marketing, aims to reach a broader audience by having active users of social media sites to share content, rather than relying on users to discover the content themselves.

Let us now see how this can be used on your Etsy platform.

SEO is the way people find your company on Etsy or search engine optimization. Have good SEO, and by directing more and more customers to your Etsy shop, Etsy will reward you. Poor SEO, right? You can miss views, far less a deal. It's an utterly critical piece of the Etsy puzzle and one that you certainly should take care of in the early stages of your Etsy store.

SEO used "keywords" (which is just a fancy way to say "one-two word phrases which define your item") to help you locate your items. Below are the keywords that you will use as well as your product summary in your titles + tags. It can also be described as a powerful tool that can help boost the visibility of your shop and item listings for sites such as Google, Bing, and Yahoo in search engine results. SEO can be tricky. Search engines also alter how words are searched, as well as the parameters for what comes up in a search. There's no way to guarantee the shop will be at the top of the search results for Google. Nonetheless, you can use some good practices to help improve the SEO of your store. You can have an Etsy shop up and running in no time, with a minimal number of clicks. Opening a store doesn't mean you're going to start making money, though.

Shoppers need to find your hand-made pieces before you can sell your hand-made pieces on Etsy. That is where Etsy SEO's importance comes in. Focusing on streamlining your Etsy listings will increase the popularity of your company. More onlookers mean more profits.

Etsy SEO is the process of increasing the exposure of your shop and its items in search engines such as Google, as well as within the search feature of Etsy itself. SEO can be challenging, especially as search engines are constantly changing the way they're searching, but Etsy sellers need to have a basic understanding of SEO best practices, so they can optimize their shops to search and get their items in front of more prospects. The search tool from Etsy is designed to provide shoppers with items they are searching for, and there are two phases of how it works: matching queries and ranking. Such variables are complex, but knowing them will help you learn how to manipulate them, helping you to attract more customers to your store. Request matching is simply how well Etsy inventory listings suit the search term for a request. When a shopper enters a search word, Etsy will filter names, tags, categories, and attributes through the listings to find the best match. Then Etsy uses details about and listing and shop to view products that shoppers are most likely to buy earlier in the results to assess the listings' rankings in search results.

Now let us go further to discuss basic factors and the "How To(s)" of Etsy SEO. The criteria that Etsy uses to rate searches include:

- **Relevance**: If a user's search term matches names, titles, categories, and attributes, listings can appear in the search results. Keywords appear higher which are an exact match.
- **Performance score ranking**: In fact, this means how good a ranking convert. To do so, Etsy is searching for clues to assess how attractive a listing is so that the more customers who visit a listing and make a

purchase can improve the rating score and placement in search results for that listing.
- **Recency:** How was the collection of products produced recently? While making a new listing, Etsy can briefly raise it in the search results to help assess the price score for the listing.
- **The score for customer and business experience**: Each shop has a score — based on customer ratings, how full the section about your shop is, and any negative feedback — that affects its rating.
- **Shipping price**: Since shipping price considerations heavily contribute to a user's buying decision, Etsy gives preference to search location to shop shipping for free or to shops offering a free shipping guarantee to shoppers in the US.
- **Translations and language**: All shop content, including the titles and tags of individual items, has to be in the language you selected when developing your Etsy account.
- **Place of the shop**: The position of the retailer is taken into account in the EU, Australia, and Canada and local goods are somewhat more prominent in search results. The place is not a consideration in other countries' searches.
- **Habits of shoppers:** Search results are often customized to individual shoppers. Etsy discovers what attracts customers, and shows them the things they are most likely to purchase.

Choose the title of a shop describing your goods.

Your shop title is a short piece of text explaining your store, so customers know what you're doing and selling, so it's one feature of your shop that you can use to influence Etsy SEO. This title will become the page title for your shop page and is the first text that a customer can see when a search engine connects to your shop, so take advantage of the opportunity to properly title your shop. Think of a title indicating what kind of products you are selling. How you name the sections of your shop can help boost the SEO of your shop too. Every section has its landing page based on the section name, with a page title. Unlike the title of your store, Etsy uses your section names to create page titles for each of the landing pages in your sections. The title page is the text that a person sees in the search engine which links to your store. Search engines show only about 66 characters for a title page, and Etsy limits section names to 24 characters. Etsy will include your shop name automatically on the title page. Specify briefly the type of items in each particular section. Using "category style" names for your sections which include your keywords not only helps a shopper navigate inside your shop but can also help shoppers find you in search engines. Etsy shop Soap making Tools, for example, sells tools for soap making.

Keyword Strategy is the Etsy SEO make-it-or-break-it

The most significant aspect is you need to think like a buyer. It sounds amazing to use keyword phrases such as "aquamarine quatrefoil pattern," but will a buyer ever look for that term? If they're like me at all, then no. By using some keyword analysis tools, you will be able to recognize easily which phrases do not resonate with consumers, what phrases do, and figure out which words to replace in to make it SEO friendly. Keywords are a big part of Amazon SEO, and it's no different from Amazon, but how do you determine which keywords are right for your shop? Next, you need to learn a little bit more about how Etsy decides how listings are put in search results. Products in the search results of Etsy must match the quest of a customer, and products that are an exact match should appear in the search results to the maximum. For example, if a shopper searches for "cat top," the search algorithm will find all products in either listing tags or titles that suit both "cat" and "top." Then, using keywords, the algorithm will put those things in the most appropriate order. Always think like a shopper when determining which keywords would do best for your search listings. If you were trying to buy a specific item or sort of object, what words would you use to look for it? Test those keywords by typing them into the search tool for Etsy to see what happens to determine if it is a good fit. You want to talk about details or long-tail keywords too. These keywords contain three or more words and are closely linked to sales because there is less competition, and users are more likely to make a purchase when they are looking for exactly what they want. For example, if you include "gold personalized name necklace" in your keywords list, users who are looking for that exact term can easily find your listing, and shoppers on the street are likely to buy one for a gold personalized name necklace.

Your Etsy Title Shop

Your shop title is a bit of a text that will appear on your shop homepage under your shop name. It can be up to 55 characters. The shop title will become the shop product's "product title," too. This is the text which a person sees in the search engine linking to your store. You can change your shop title by going to the Shop Manager and clicking under Sales Channels on the pencil icon next to your shop name. We recommend explaining your shop briefly, as well as the things you sell. Some sellers do a slogan or tag line. When future customers are likely to look for you this way, consider using your full name or company name in your store title.

Don't be imaginative with Titles

You are a talented and exclusive company owner, as a seller on Etsy. Whilst allowing your imagination to expand product names can be appealing, if you don't, it's better. It makes a very unsuccessful word, a common mistake with Etsy sellers. People shopping for goods aren't going to use cutesy or excessively imaginative terms. For example, if you sell original paintings you don't want to put your painting's unique name into the title. Instead use words such as "abstract painting, acrylic on canvas" in your title and save the title of the painting for an explanation of the product.

Have a very great product.

The first step to drawing in shoppers is to deliver something special, interesting, and desirable. When deciding whether to automate your SEO search or not, take a look at the items in your shop and consider what makes your item or product different from those of everyone else. If you want to improve your shop's look and feel, find out more about how to do that here.

Think like a shopper

Some handy Etsy applications can uncover the right keywords, and in a little bit, we'll get to them. But put yourself in the shoes of your clients, before that. You'll be able to quickly identify the right words and phrases to use in your listings when you understand your customers and know why they're looking for your items. It would also aid when dealing with keyword analysis from the technical side. Etsy SEO software can create long lists of keywords and lots of options that can take time to arrange and sift through. Knowing the customers and their search goals promote the cycle of keyword analysis because you already have an understanding of what customers are searching for and how to create it.

CHAPTER SIX:

Using SEO and keywords properly in your title and description to rank at the top.

Learning SEO is important if traffic and brand recognition is to increase significantly. To stay on top of SEO takes a lot of work and creativity. Google's algorithms are constantly updated so staying tuned to the latest news is critical. Having that in mind, you will become your SEO expert, with a bit of practice. It is a possible task to increase the popularity of your brand on Etsy and it primarily depends on two crucial factors: SEO optimization of your Etsy store and, of course, the care of your shop's graphics business. That's why we're going to share some valuable Etsy SEO tips and tricks today which will help boost your brand's ranking on the website. When you wonder how to increase your brand's exposure on Etsy, you need to split your promotional strategies into two separate but complementary levels: on the one hand, you need to logically reason to position yourself on search engines like Google, while on the other hand, you need to think about your users and their needs as well and above all. It is a basic concept that does not accept exceptions: it would be very difficult to raise market awareness of your company if you do not take care of all aspects at the same time.

Keywords, besides having SEO water, show even more about users and what they are dealing with. When a buyer scans, his algorithm does two things to decide the outcomes shoppers see. They are as follows:

Matching demand

Etsy kicks things off with a process called query matching in which it runs through listings and collects those which suit the search query of the customer. Etsy achieves so by considering:

- Names
- Terms
- Groups
- Attribute

Ranking

Upon the matching of requests, Etsy rates all matched listings based on the probability of each buyer to purchase the products. During this step Etsy takes into account the following rating factors:

- Listing relevance. Etsy looks at the title, descriptions, categories, and attributes of a product, and tries to find out how they are matched with the buyer's quest. The closest you are to the match, the higher you are.
- The listing consistency. To calculate a metric called the "listing quality score," Etsy looks at the conversions of a listing. The higher the conversion rate, the higher the listing score and rating.
- The Listing Age. New listings are having a small temporary increase in rankings. This boost may last for several hours or days, depending on the search volume of the product. In turn, this helps Etsy to understand how shoppers communicate with each listing, which will then affect its quality score for listing.
- Customer feedback and feedback at the company. Etsy provides a seamless browsing and purchasing experience for the customers. To do so, their search engine factors in the history of a seller's customer service as well as the shop's content, including its About page, store policies, ratings, and feedback. Etsy then scores shops by ranking their listings favorably in search results, based on the experience they offer and rewards high-scoring sellers.
- Costs on freight. To customers the shipping price is important, so it's important to Etsy. According to a company-led report, shoppers are 50 percent less likely to purchase an item if they find the shipping price to be higher than what they are used to. For this reason, shipping costs are now an Etsy ranking factor. Sellers with lower shipping costs — or, even better, those offering free shipping — will typically see their listings in search results rank higher.

- Language and translation. If you are selling to foreign customers, adding custom translations to your listings will help. Although Etsy automatically translates listings to suit the question and language settings of each customer, the manual translation of your content can help it outstrip automatically translated listings. It is because manual translations also sound more natural, and are more in line with the traditional way in which buyers will type their queries.
- Context-Specific (CSR) Ratings. Also factored in the Etsy rankings are the browsing behavior of a buyer — including which products they clicked on and items they previously purchased. Etsy uses Context Specific Ranking technology to serve personalized search results and endeavors to give each buyer the most relevant listings depending on their past behavior.

Attributes

Attributes are the more information you might use to identify the goods. They are shown on the left side of the search results page and can be used by customers to narrow down the search results. Attributes serve two purposes: they facilitate the lives of buyers by allowing them to filter search results, and they allow Etsy to more effectively match queries. Through having as many specific attributes as possible when you apply for your listing you can maximize this aspect of your listing. For example, if you're selling a pair of black leather ballet flats then you'd pick attributes like "flats," "black," and "leather." You can also use them to extend your listing's matching potential. The more important qualities you have, the greater the product's chances of turning up on search results. Let's just say you use "violet" to describe a shirt you're selling. You could add "purple" as a color attribute to enhance your ranking chances because it still accurately describes the item.

Groups

Although Etsy categories are mainly used to help shoppers browse the web and narrow down their search, they continue to play a significant role in SEO. Categories and sub-categories act as Etsy tags, and the web uses them to search queries when matching the listings. Optimize the categories by making them as descriptive as possible. First go to the sub-categories when classifying your pieces, as Etsy immediately applies your goods to the larger categories in which the sub-category is nestled. For example, if you sell a ring with several stones, then use the "Multi-tone Rings" sub-category. If you do so, the product will be classified automatically under "Rings" and "Jewelry & Accessories," and shoppers can still find your items as they search for those categories.

Find the best Etsy Keywords

Keywords are the cornerstones of your Etsy SEO strategy. Once reviewing a buyer's search query, the first thing Etsy does is browse through its listing inventory to find the ones that best fit the user's search words.

Use Etsy SEO tools to find the volume and ideas for keyword searches

Etsy keyword tools can be used to get even more feedback on search terms and to decide which queries to prioritize. Check out Etsy solutions and apps below to find the best keywords. Scout Keywords begin by reviewing your Etsy listings. It then provides you with tips on which SEO errors you need to correct like missing images or tags, or too short descriptions. Keyword Scout can also be used to do keyword analysis. Just enter a word or phrase that best describes your niche, and a list of the most common related Etsy tags will be created by Keyword Scout. Using such tags to refine current product lists, or generate new ideas.

Look at the analytics on Etsy

Another way to come up with keywords? Test your files on Etsy. The native reporting tool provided by Etsy provides valuable insights into how people find your listings. Apart from showing page views and sources of traffic, Etsy also displays the search words that contributed to your listings.

Optimize key parts of the listing

After understanding which keywords to use, include them in your listing. When matching requests, Etsy takes a look at the listing components below to see if they are matched with the quest of a customer. Go through them and see to it that they are search optimized.

Heading Name

Etsy lets you use up to 140 characters in your title but gives the first few words more weight. So, first, make sure you enter the keywords most relevant. When you sell original paintings, you can use words such as "wall art," "office painting" or "abstract painting" instead of the title of the piece — you can save it for the definition of the work. Look at this illustration, where the seller uses in the listing title search-friendly words like "initial wall art" and "bird painting," but saves the title of the artwork — "Never Alone" — for the description.

Etsy Tags

Etsy tags have two functions: help customers discover identical or related items and assist Etsy with the process of matching queries. Etsy lets you add up to 13 tags each time you list them, so make them count! Vary the tags so that they cover a range of search words. For example, if you sell earrings, add tags like "custom jewelry" or "women's gifts" in addition to typical tags like "diamond earrings" or "gold earrings." Etsy tags can be up to 20 characters long and have several words in them. Etsy also suggests using multi-word tags (e.g., "handmade earrings" vs. "handmade") as they allow you to be more specific. Long-tail keywords should be given preference over generic names, too. Why? For what? And when searching for items shoppers who know what they want usually enter different search words. Use those long-tail keywords lets you get ahead of those clients.

Spice up your listing material

Getting a listing that aligns with a buyer's quest is a good start, but it isn't the only deciding factor in search results ranking high. Although a keyword-optimized listing is a must, it is equally critical to have good visuals and copy because these are items that contribute to conversions. As stated earlier, when deciding their position in the search results, Etsy's algorithm factors in the conversion rate for a query. The more people who click on a listing and then purchase the item, the higher the quality score of the listing will be. This, in effect, raises ranks for you.

Collect several comments and reviews

97% of customers read feedback online before purchasing. That is not to come as a surprise. Online shoppers love input from other customers, particularly if they buy something that they can't see and touch in person. This is why your listings must include ratings and reviews. The good news is Etsy is already helping you out on this front — it instantly nudges consumers to share their product reviews. Try inserting a note in your packages thanking your customers and asking them to review their purchase to take a step further in motivating customers to rate and review your products. Only be careful of the wording. Offering extra products, facilities, or rewards in return for feedback is contradictory to Etsy laws, so you want to make sure your note doesn't come off as pushy.

Using high-quality photos

Etsy allows you to add up to 10 photos per listing so take the opportunity to present your products in the best light possible. Add photographs of your items being used, in addition to taking pictures from different angles. If appropriate, provide photos that give people a better understanding of the size, texture, and so on of the piece.

Write descriptions which are clear and informational

Although Etsy's search algorithm doesn't check product reviews, they play an important role in through sales — which then increases the Etsy rankings. In your product description, Etsy has no word count limit, and the length of the post can depend on how complicated your product is, or how much of a story you want to say.

First, write to humans, then to search engines.

It has been found that more and more bloggers and content developers are returning to the old SEO process, where keywords intended to push search results outperformed the real quality of engaging, useful content. If that's you, it's high time to change your mindset. Don't give preference to search engines over actual people reading your job. Instead write user content, people who have eyes to read, and credit cards to buy your stuff. Search spiders are just scripts — they're not buying products, they 're not engaging with you on social media, and they're not going to become loyal clients.

Further discussed, to improve your brand's exposure on Etsy, you do need to learn how to catch potential customers' interest and turn them into actual customers. Here, the quality of your e-commerce's graphics sector plays a very important role: the photographs are taken professionally come straight to the beholder's heart, as they communicate great emotions along with the message your brand wants to convey. You'll have to think like a window designer might think to sell on Etsy: use bright colors, shoot with models, and try to do it in dynamic positions and maybe use a background that would be familiar to your primary target. The only limit is your creativity: the more your images catch the customer, the more items you can sell on Etsy.

High shipping costs may deter buyers from completing their procurement process. Etsy has identified the price of shipments as a ranking element, so creating affordable shipping rates, including "free shipping," will improve the results of your positioning. The attributes that you add to your listings often serve as tags and can help you locate your items in the search results. The attributes describe specific product characteristics, such as colors, occasions, measurements, etc.

At the beginning of the title, putting the most appropriate keywords will let the customer know exactly what the product you are selling is, resulting in more clicks, likes, and thus more sales. The tags and titles must be in the language you choose when opening your shop. Adding tags in other languages does not make your search results show up in your products. Etsy can automatically translate the headings and marks into the language of the customer.

Completing your store's "about section" can help you increase your "customer & market experience score," thus improving your search results ranking. To Etsy, making sellers share their stories is important as they can build a special bond with customers and make them feel comfortable. With consistent policies, customers will know what to expect if they purchase in your shop, empowering them with greater protection and confidence. Additionally, having transparent and consistent policies in your store will improve your "customer & business experience ranking" and also help you gain more exposure in the community

In conclusion, Etsy recommends that you test your new strategies and periodically revise your statistics. Ok, you can track which items and keywords drive your store's most traffic. And then you can update those low-performance listings as well, and you can add other items that will further expand your bid.

CHAPTER SEVEN:

Hidden features of Etsy can provide you the most powerful boost in search engine rankings.

Businesses are searching for ways to tailor their offerings to better align with global trends. You can get a personalized shirt with your dog's face on it, with the internet at your fingertips, and even have a shirt for your dog with your name on it. This is just one example of the increasing culture of customization and interest in the strange that has sprung up, creating an increase in the amount of Etsy stores out there. Whether customers search on Etsy or Google, optimizing your Etsy store and products can help you stay visible. Here are the simple tips and tricks to help improve your Etsy shop and product listings to raise Google's traffic for sales. Understanding your customer's keyword for your own company is beyond important and will help you locate future customers and fans. Marmalead is a perfect resource for the Etsy shops to locate keywords. You can use it to type in a tag (or keyword) and see total results or competing products and shops, total views, average weekly views, average weekly favorites, and much more.

Ever wondered, what's Etsy SEO? What does your Etsy Rating decide? How performs the algorithm behind your listing ranking? And what are the variables that affect the top of Etsy's quest for your Etsy listings? Those are among some of the top questions that Etsy sellers should and must find answers to. The latest statistics from Statistics indicate a growing fondness for 'Esty's most innovative and fresh marketplace. Among the surfeit of other markets offering many more choices, Etsy ranks at the top, making it the first choice among all budding sellers. Sellers' primary concern is how to get the Etsy listings on the first search results page. As per the Etsy Seller Handbook, when it comes to Etsy listing rating it depends solely on the Etsy SEO.

Label & Name

Speak of Etsy as Google. Much like the latter, the tags and titles used in descriptions of the product must match the term or phrase sought by the buyer. If the search terms are not present, the result does not include the product. While you might not be in charge of some of the ranking criteria, this one is absolute. Doing a little research and curating the description of the product which includes the title, tags, attributes and specifications should be the first thing you do before you get the products listed.

Here are some of the fast tips to help you tailor a result-driven overview of the items:

- The title of the product should be searchable. The exact term of the phrase is given a higher priority. So, keep a check on the vendors selling the same product description. Create the headlines on a similar line.
- Provide the tags and product summary with other related keywords and long-tail query terminology. Etsy lets you have 13 keywords included. So, you should make sure you leave no marks behind.
- The title character limit is 140 characters, but only the first 55 characters will appear in the search result, so the keywords will appear at the top. In Google ranking, this will help as well as may even help if it is integrated with Google Shopping.
- The tags shall also be considered by the Etsy search engine, along with the names. There is commercial and deliberate significance to these search words. So, make sure you wisely opt for the tags.

Product Quality Listing

The more clicks like, or buys an object, the greater its chances of doing well in the search result. It is regarded as 'price of display.' New stores and the new releases, however, have a neutral rating score and do not affect the placement. In this respect, Etsy has an automatic approach. The added products on Etsy that are gaining more attention, i.e. the products that are gaining more clicks will be added more times to the favorite list and will be given preference for high conversion rates. Make sure you sell exclusive goods, and the service you give to the customers is strong.

Below are some of the tips you need to look after in this regard:

- Ensure that when using your product, the buyers get relative to experience.
- Good product reviews have an advantage over the rivals on the web pages.
- Your store's About Us section and the seller's policy must be clear. That can also ensure that the search results are put in Etsy.
- The cost can be one of the factors contributing to low-clicks. Stop pricing certain goods too low or too high. Do some study on a rival in this regard and come up with a suitable solution.

Considering the growing urge of sellers to get to the top of Etsy search, Etsy has come up with useful SEO tips and various websites such as Etsy and Marmalead testing for the best keywords and optimizing Etsy search engines. For the buyer's question, the right and reliable implementation of Etsy SEO is the secret for achieving the top spot on the Etsy search page. When you pay careful attention to your search engine optimization strategies, you will guarantee a strong Etsy rating for your company.

Various factors affect the ranking of a listing, one factor is working on keywords which is totally in your control and can be improved almost immediately. Sellers should think like a buyer when choosing Keywords. You will find whatever search query possibilities a buyer may bring into the store. Various tools are available to get the best match for keywords, and you can also evaluate which keywords to find as the best keyword to list.

Etsy and Marmalead are some of the methods for better keyword collection. On the other side, you can go to the Etsy search bar and Etsy search analytics, if you want to go for organic choices. These keywords should be incorporated into each listing aspect that includes Title Listing, Tags, Item Description, and Product Attributes. Etsy search algorithm takes the visitors' search term and combines them with the text in Name, Item Description, and Tags, suggesting results accordingly.

Mastering the consistency and optimization of content

Content is the king-pin of all that is represented on the internet. In terms of views, shares, downloads, and conversions, quality content typically draws full limelight. Etsy content is not limited to textual components, but it takes into account three essential things, namely: product illustration, product description, and product reviews.

Here Etsy rewards certain high performing listings which means they get more visits; they are added to favorite lists and they are purchased daily. It was described by Etsy as a price listing.

The products that receive higher views will be given preference; will be added to the favorite list more frequently and will have high conversion rates. The explanations have particular significance in increasing consumer interaction, thus improving customer purchases along with the positive/negative product feedback.

Regular Updates

Etsy's search algorithm tends to check out the newly modified goods. It takes into account the way an object has been listed or relisted recently. Regularly update the product details, the title, and the tags. Keep the content updated and fresh with time.

Shop Location

Etsy search considers the vendor's shop location and this increases visibility in search results. When checks are carried out in other nations, then the shop location may not be considered. The positioning of the shop makes the store famous and results in higher product rankings. The shipping profile can even be updated on Etsy. The rationale behind that is to ensure online shoppers are delivered faster. Third-party vendors have no control over it.

Artificial Intelligence

As per Etsy, their search system is now attempting to highlight, based on certain factors, "results that are most relevant to the specific buyer." Such variables may be daylight time, desires, and others. This can help shoppers get precise search results but it's quite a barrier for vendors. This is because any time you type into a database, they will no longer see the same results. Even if they make the searches in the incognito mode, they won't get the same result. With the latest technology coming into play, tracking the search results have become quite an issue for the Etsy sellers.

Listing Language

When you sign up on Etsy, it's important to list the products in the shop language to sell your products. All the listing information of a product should be in the native language of a Marketplace. For example, if a Marketplace works on the French language then the English keywords would not be recognized by the search algorithm of that Marketplace. All the listing information of the product should be in the Etsy Marketplace language only otherwise it will never help to bring up your items.

Relevant linking:

Links play an important role in higher search engine ranking. It is a great idea to link your shop page with the product and policies listed at the Etsy Marketplace. The shop page information should contain the following information:

- Shop Name
- Shop Description
- Sales Count
- Start Date

The shop page information available at the Marketplace will promote the brand and enhance visibility which will ultimately bring more traffic towards the store.

Discussing further, Etsy has made it easier for craftsmen and artisans than ever to take advantage of their talent. But to be a good Etsy seller, you need to do more than just set up a shop. If you want to stand out from the rivals you must practice entrepreneurial skills. Sale on Etsy is playing numbers, and the more people you consider your offering, the greater your chances of a sale! You can push traffic through social media posts or ads but you can draw customers 24/7 by optimizing your store for the hunt. Like every other search engine, Etsy has a mathematical equation for the search ranking results. You will boost product rankings if you understand the inputs, and how often they appear. Sellers should be aware that Etsy has made some significant changes to its SEO algorithm this year.

One of the most important things any Etsy seller has to do is increase the views their listings are getting. More insights mean more profits. Etsy Views are the number of users that visit your shop and listings over a set date range. You want the target audience and future buyers to pull in searches so that your Etsy search engine optimization needs to be satisfactory. Other means of raising views include social media promotion, blogging, and networking. Implementing a keyword strategy may at first seem frustrating and monotonous, but it will gradually become routine and will yield results.

Knowing how people are looking for and seeing your shop and goods is important for performing well as increasing the custom market. When it comes to SEO, try thinking first like a human and second like a search engine. No matter what you're selling, take a few minutes to think about how on a search engine you'd be looking for your product, and then use the tools and tips to create a plan. When you understand your target, and how to meet them, a competitive room is not a bad thing.

Add new articles

When you don't do anything else, adding new items is the single most unbelievably successful way to increase your shop's views and sales every time. But, if the idea of creating new products to put in your shop makes you break out in hives then that's no shame! Etsy loves stores that are introducing new products. Whenever there's a new listing in a store. That boost isn't permanent — but you can improve its efficacy by introducing products you know there's a demand for (i.e. you've got consumers that love buying similar things from your shop), and turning them into sales — you simply need to make those regular sales of that item to keep it boosted.

Connect this product to the current one

Is there a mix of colors or custom design requests you get a lot of requests for? Perhaps it is time to think about adding that to the store! I've always considered my customers to be some of my best idea creators and if I've already developed an item with some modifications for previous customers, it's not so hard to add it to my store! Never feel like you need to build something new from scratch — look at what works for you and improve on it.

Bundle the items

This is one of the "up-sell" hacks that work well. Accept that shoppers are very lazy people and market the shop accordingly (I know I'm when I shop online!). Yes, you may be offering 3 kitchen-themed art prints in your shop, but what are the chances of a shopper searching all over your store to find matches to the one he/she already has in their cart? Not well.

Center your Social Media weekly around launching your product

Schedule a few updates on social media about your product drops (multiple updates on the first two days of the launch, then spread out here and there for the next week), and be sure to send an email to your list (and if you don't have one, get one installed! I'm using Convert Kit and I love it) announcing the decrease. Repetition is key here. Don't just mention it once and cross your fingers— you're going to be sorely deceived. A couple of posts and emails about a product drop means that they'll read the news more than once and think about it.

Reviews affect on SEO

Customer reviews are subjects that indirectly affect the optimization of the Etsy Search Engine. Sellers with good reviews and a large number of comments also hit the top of the results page of the app. Etsy overlooks which sellers get the higher conversions. While it also considers what and how much feedback they are receiving in terms of ratings and reviews. You will also need to consider obtaining more commitments to your listings. Optimize your listings in such a way that they are most relevant and it seems to be unique and exciting. Such product reviews also help to achieve good ratings, so you shouldn't ignore this important factor when planning your listings to get search results on the first page.

It has changed so much of our world forever

As marketers, it is our job to help leverage the tools available to us. It is especially true for ads on search engines. Where we have the opportunity to understand how our products are being felt by consumers and the interactions, they want from us to understand how they are looking. This data is useful not only for search campaigns but also for the business strategy. Search results can help inform strategic decisions about store locations, hours, forms of payment, and so much so that your company will make better and more educated decisions on how to succeed. You should understand that the point of viewing your stats is to see what works, and either does more if there is room in you to schedule OR to learn a new way of driving views. For instance, if I wanted to increase my views, I bet I could do that by trying at least a little on Facebook, but as that's no fun for me, I don't! Figure out what you're good at, and start working to drive up your shop's views!

Listing number in your shop

Etsy usually has plenty of users voicing complaints on the seller's website and wondering why they're not getting more views. Usually what Etsy does is ask to see their shop, and they have 6-10 listings. And of course, they have not many thoughts. Now that's just 10 chances of getting found in search. The best thing about this one is that by listing more, you can change the number.

Growing positive feedback

This one looks ready to use but I wouldn't. Yes, you can include a small card asking for a great review in your packages, but overall, you'll get about 20-25 percent of your customers leaving reviews. The more you sell, the greater that number will grow. I'm not so sure that I'd mess with this too much, maybe selling more!

You got more customers in the past

Getting clients here helps! On the "home page" Etsy reveals items from your favorite shops and past sales and in the emails, they send out. This is frustrating as you can't get this until someone buys, and until they see your listing you can't get someone to buy it. Please be vigilant!

You've sold things in the past

The more stuff you sell the more stuff you'll get. I know this seems to be crazy hard if you don't sell anything right now, but Etsy rewards shops selling things. You can control this a little by doing promotions on social media, emailing your list, or using a site like Etsy On Sale to manage your discounts (promo link, you'll get credits to try a free sale!)

CHAPTER EIGHT:

Best way to price your products

Ask customers to pay your product or service too much and they will stop buying. Say too little and your reports on the profit margin or consumers conclude that your product is low quality. An 'optimum size' factor in all of your prices, while staying appealing to consumers, maximizes your margins. Here's how you can set the rates. Pricing your goods is one of the biggest decisions that you are going to make, as it affects almost every aspect of your business. Your pricing is a key factor in anything from your cash flow to your profit margins, on whether you can afford to pay expenses. That's why when you launch a new store or product — even before you write down your product descriptions — it's all too easy to get stuck on pricing but it's important not to let the decision stop you from launching. The best pricing data you can get is from getting started and tested with real clients. One of the keys to success in business is the proper pricing of the goods. Rightly pricing your goods, and that will improve how much you sell, providing the basis for a profitable business. Get your pricing plan wrong and you may be generating issues your company will never solve. Various types of pricing strategies occur in the industry. There is no single surefire, formula-based solution, however, that fits all kinds of goods, businesses or markets. Pricing your product usually involves considering some key factors, including identifying your target customer, tracking how many competitors are charging, and understanding the quality-price relationships. The good news is that you have a lot of flexibility in how you set the rates. Product pricing is an essential component in determining your product or service's success, yet eCommerce entrepreneurs and businesses often consider pricing only as an afterthought. They settle and use the first price that comes to mind, copy or (even worse) guess competitors.

When you start selling products in your Etsy store, you might be wondering how you can decide how much your customers will pay. If you're planning to run a successful Etsy store, you've got to feel confident doing some math,

(Materials + Overhead + Labor) x 2 = Wholesale price

Wholesale price x 2 = demand for retail

- Know business. Learn consumer. You need to figure out how much consumers will pay, and how much rivals will be paying. Instead, you may try to equal or beat them. It's risky to simply match a price, though you need to be sure that all your costs-direct and indirect-are protected.
- Use the right approach to price. Cost-plus pricing includes applying a percentage of mark-up to costs; this can differ across goods, companies, and sectors. Pricing based on value is determined by how much value your clients add to your product. Until making an estimate, determine what your pricing policy is.
- Figure your costs out. Include all direct costs including money spent on product or service production. So, measure the variable costs (for products, shipping, and so on)-the higher it would be, the better you produce or sell. Figure out what proportion of the fixed costs the company has to pay (overheads such as rents, premiums, and wages). Add all those costs together and divide by volume to create a break-even unit figure.
- Make pricing the cost-plus. For your break-even point, you will need to add a margin or markup. This is usually expressed as a break-even percentage. Industry standards, experience, or knowledge of the market can help you determine the markup stage. If the price looks too high, cut costs and lower the price accordingly. Be mindful of the cost-plus price limitations, as it operates under the premise that you are going to sell all units. When you are not, then your income would be smaller.
- Set a price basing on demand. To set a price based on demand you would need to know your business well. The cost of bringing a hairdryer to the market, for example, could be £ 10. But if this is the market value you could charge £ 25 to customers.
- Just think of other factors. How will the VAT charge affect the price? Can you hold small margins on some goods to get higher margin profits on others? You can need to measure different prices for the various regions, markets, or online sales that you produce. Do you need customers to allow for possible late payment? Consider your terms of payment, and keep an eye on your cash flow.
- Stick to your toes. Prices are seldom fixable for long. This will increase your costs, buyers, and rivals, and you'll need to adjust

your prices to keep up with the demand. Keep an eye on what's going on and speak frequently with your customers to ensure your rates remain optimum.

Let's assume, for example, that you have built a product with the following costs:

Price of content = $20

Job expenses = $10

Overhead = $8

Total price = $38

Rising rates and crickets

If you are an experienced seller who re-evaluates your prices but is afraid that no one in your shop would want to pay higher prices, you should understand that price increases are just a fact of life. Recently, Amazon prime increased its price and, if they have to do so as a big company, smaller companies certainly are no different. Rising rates are just a part of being a practical business owner a lot of times. There doesn't have to be a rise of 40 percent. This could be a few bucks added here and there. Many sellers risk being separated from their current customers, which is a legitimate concern.

Be clear about your profits

The first move is to make your selling plan very transparent on what you want to achieve: you want to make money. Therefore, you own a company. Making money means producing enough revenue from the selling of your goods that you can not only cover your expenses but also make a profit and maybe expand your business.

Now, if in your shop you sell goods, that's your work. It's not something you just love to make anymore. So, it is big to make the mental shift from hobby to business. Making this change can also specifically slow down sellers as regards pricing. It's important to get this right as soon as you can, not just for yourself, but for everyone concerned. There will always be someone who can sell what you are selling for less, or something similar. Any way. Whatever. No matter how small your item is priced, it will still be sold for less by somebody.

Pricing first, then volume

It doesn't make sense to want to bid for the lowest price when you think of it this way. Note, many buyers don't try the lowest price item anyway. Bottom line: if you're not successful and want to be, and you want to be in business as well, you will make the right amount. You have no alternative. This begins at selling first and then the number of sales is secondary to that. What happened was that she got exhausted because she didn't make enough to keep up with the amount of time, she put in to do all that research. You Ought NOT to get into such a situation. Price right to start so that no matter what happens, you know that you're going to make a profit.

Few revenues, greater profit

It is where you get into play with knowing the numbers inside and out. Whether you've just increased rates and seen profits fall, it doesn't have to mean you're making less money. If you're pricing right, you could experience fewer sales but more benefits. It means that for more money you're doing less work which is the sweet spot of sales!

Defining labor costs

Calculating the labor costs allows you to set an hourly rate for your time first. Make sure you're paying a decent wage — one that accounts for the talent you need to craft your piece. Think about how much you want to make for your money, or need to. (This factor is especially important if you want to leave your day job.) Most skilled craftsmen go from $12 to $20 an hour in the neighborhood. Armed with your hourly wage, you're able to make your labor costs work out. Such expenses have to take into account the time needed to do the following:

- Design a piece
- Get part supplies
- Create the piece
- Photograph this piece
- Build the item list for that piece, including the title and description of the item
- Package and supply piece

Moving the head up

They want to compensate for your depreciation, in addition to estimating your supplies and labor costs. The overhead may include as follows:

- Tools and equipment used for producing the goods
- Department Deliveries
- Packaging supplies
- Utilities (for example, link to the internet, electricity used, sewing machine, etc.)
- Etsy Fees
- Fees to PayPal

Pricing targeted to the market

Business-oriented pricing is often referred to as a competitive pricing strategy, which compares related goods (competition) on the business, which then depends on how well their product suits the seller causing them to set the price higher or lower than their rivals.

- Price above market: pricing your product deliberately above the competition to label yourself as getting a higher-quality or better-performing product
- The market for copies: Sell your item at the same price as your competition to maximize profit while remaining competitive
- Priced below the market: Using data as a benchmark and pricing a product consciously below its competitors to attract customers to your store above theirs

Each of the aforementioned market-oriented strategies has its pros and cons. With market-oriented pricing, to price your product accurately, it is important to understand the costs of making your product, as well as the quality compared to the competitors.

Dynamic pricing, also referred to as demand pricing or time-based pricing, is a strategy in which businesses set flexible prices based on current market demands for a product or service. In other words, dynamic pricing is the act of changing a price several times over the day, week, or month to better match consumer buying habits. It is not just services such as Uber that benefit from dynamic pricing to maximize profits. For big eCommerce shopping days like Black Friday and Cyber Monday, Amazon has long been using price surges on its most competitive items.

Add variable expenses (per product)

Above all, you need to consider all the costs involved with getting any product out of the door.

If you order your products, you will receive a straightforward reply as to how much each unit costs you, which is the cost of the goods sold.

If you're making your products, you'll have to dig a little deeper and look at a bundle of raw materials. How much does it cost, and how many products can you create out of it? That will provide you with a rough estimate of the cost of the goods sold per item.

You shouldn't forget, though, that the time you spend on your company is also worthwhile. Set an hourly rate you want to receive from your company to reward your time, and then divide it by how many items you will produce in that time. To set a sustainable price, ensure that the cost of your time is incorporated as a variable cost of the product.

Here's a sample list of costs that you might incur on any product.

- Commodity price sold $3.25
- Operating time $2.00
- Packing up $1.78
- promotional materials $0.75
- Shipping $4.50
- Affiliate contributes $2.00
  Total cost per product: $14.28

Add a margin to profit

Once you have a total number per product sold for your variable costs, it's time to build profit into your price.

Let's assume you want your goods to gain a gross margin of 20 percent in addition to the variable costs. It's important to remember two things when choosing this percentage.

The fixed expenses have not yet been listed, and you'll have costs to pay beyond just the variable costs.

You need to consider the overall market and make sure that your price with this margin still falls within your market's overall "acceptable" price. If you're 2x the price of all your competitors, sales might become challenging depending on your category of products.

Take your total variable costs and divide them by 1 minus your desired profit margin, expressed as a decimal, once you're ready to calculate a price. For a profit margin of 20 percent, that's 0.2, so you'd divide your cost of a variable by 0.8.

In this scenario, this will give you a $17.85 base price for your product which you can round up to $18.00.

Don't forget about cost fixes

Bear in mind that variable costs aren't the only costs.

Fixed costs are the expenses you'd pay no matter what, and stay the same whether you're selling 10 products or 1000. These are a vital part of running your company and the goal is that they are not protected by sales of your product.

It can be difficult to find out how your fixed costs fit into when you pick a per-unit amount. In a break-even calculator spreadsheet, an easy way to do this is to take the details about variable costs you've already obtained and set them up. Go to Tab > Create a copy to save a duplicate that is only available to you to edit the spreadsheet.

This is designed to look at the fixed costs and variable costs in one place and see how many units you will have to sell to break even at the chosen price. Such calculations will enable you to make an educated decision about the balance between covering your fixed costs and setting a fair and sustainable price.

CHAPTER NINE:

How to stay organized

Being organized can be quite the hectic work, but you need to understand that your customers do not want to keep looking for things in your shop just because you did not put it in the right place, or just because it is not where it usually is. Consistency and precision are key here and precision is key here.

Arranging the order of things in your shop carefully is a perfect way to entice customers to browse your goods. The way your items are displayed in your Etsy shop will make a major impression on your brand, just like a show in a physical store! When you make your first sale on Etsy, thinking about getting so many orders to fill that be your mind's furthest thing. But for many sellers, one of the trickiest aspects of running a company is to keep up with demand as sales ramp up. Setting up inventory management systems and supporting advanced planning is one way to make busy times more manageable. Etsy lets you organize by section your pieces. What if everything was set haphazardly when you went to your grocery store—with the milk alongside the charcoal briquettes, the kitty litter next to the radishes, the sardines' cheese? You'd never find something you wanted to buy! The grocery stores are also divided into sections and aisles. Why is your Etsy shop any different? For example, if you're selling various types of items — say, magnets, notebooks, and image frames — you can use sections to organize your shop by item. Even if you don't sell different types of products — maybe you're all about knit caps — you can use sections to arrange your goods by, say, type of yarn, size, or quality. Ten sections in all, as well as the default All Items section which is available in each shop, are required. You have to straighten shelves and store products all day long to make sure that the next batch of buyers will still find them appealing and potentially get you sales. Such repetitive activity can be tedious and takes a lot of your time, but organizing is a fundamental job that keeps your site smooth and appealing, keeping customers on your site longer. Etsy comes with so many apps to help you boost your store. Shop sections are great because they allow you to organize your listings by theme, color, size, type of object, etc. We can be quickly edited, rearranged, and removed, giving your store more flexibility.

- Be consistent in the theme and imagery.
- Seasonally change the arrangements to fit the shopping patterns.
- Keep a complete shop to prevent sparse looks.
- Using the best thumbnail picture for every single product.

You might begin to question "why is it important" to be organized. I mean I could as well just put it all up whichever way and still get my sales. Well, the truth is nobody wants to deal with a wardrobe that is not well arranged especially when it is not yours. Let us see some practical reasons why being organized is necessarily important.

To make browsing easy for shoppers

Shop Sections allow visitors to look at your product range easily online. For example, if someone visits my store to look for geometric earrings, they can simply select "Earrings" to save time on the left-hand side. I also sometimes paste a link back to a section of my Etsy store at the bottom of a related page. Through checking your Shop Stats, you will check to see if shoppers are browsing your Parts, which will alert you when they move through.

To help your shop remain in shape

They're also a fast and convenient way to streamline your Etsy shop's maintenance. When you are searching for a particular item listed in your shop, use the Sections to narrow down the list. In this way, the function is really useful for sellers, besides buyers as we have just mentioned.

Sharing on social media is done easily

Sections make bundling like items together really easy and you can then share them on social media platforms. Only click on your publicly available Etsy marketplace section and then copy the URL in the top window. Using these clickable links in the URL section to support a community of items you have in your Facebook, Twitter, and more in your store.

To promote products on sale

Finally, you can use the Parts to support your sale or clearing goods. This is great for products you would like to discount because they haven't sold or those you discontinued. Create a segment labeled "Clearance," "Sale," or "Last Chance" to draw shoppers to the bargain. You can only put a listing in one line, so these things will not be included in your store along with the other related types of goods.

How will we go about all this then?

Track your times

I used to believe, like many business owners, that being extremely busy and overextended is proof of being productive. But just because you are sitting in front of a computer doesn't mean you're getting things that are done that are important. Upon doing a brief review of how I was spending my working hours, I found that about 40 percent of my time was spent on busy work and non-essential jobs. I set out to make a change.

Break down your To-Do list

I'm making two lists to split my job into manageable chunks: a large weekly to-do-list, and a smaller regular task list. Breaking the large list down into smaller bits keeps me inspired. I don't feel stressed, so by doing smaller, more manageable things I can make a dent in larger projects.

Prioritize the night before

When you plan for tomorrow's workday, recognize three things you need to accomplish on your daily to-do list. Those are important things you should be paying full attention to. When I started defining three top tasks for each day, remaining focused on them became simpler and coping with less important problems when the time allowed.

Determine when you are best at work

Since I'm not a morning person, I schedule boring activities earlier in the day, such as printing and shipping. I save more thought-intensive jobs, as I prefer to do my best work later in the day or late at night.

By comparison, if you find that first thing in the morning is most successful, use that time to knock off the most difficult things on your list.

Establish a daily work routine

Although it may seem counter-intuitive, it is important for all business owners, including innovative entrepreneurs, to have a strict daily routine. Since at any given moment I always like to leap at whatever tasks my imagination hits, I try hard to keep to a plan. It's important to be precise. For instance, instead of planning to "get up earlier" to start my working day, I make it a goal to "wake up at 6 a.m." If you work hard to stick to a daily routine, eventually you can turn any behavior into a working habit.

Place the boundaries

I used to work into the early hours of the morning, thinking this was the only way to quickly turn the job around and keep my clients satisfied. Soon, my clients came to expect that from me. Now, I keep the working hours set and I shut down everything when the time is up. I do so out of respect for myself and my family, my two sons included. I also find that I have to unplug from all my work to be recharged to return to it. Surprisingly enough my clients now enjoy my time more.

Get yourself confident saying "No! When you're having a hard time keeping up with what you've already set out to do, say "no" on the way through any other inquiries.

In getting chummy with this two-letter word, you will be compelled to commit to just certain things that you are completely confident you can do. When anyone approaches me with a new idea or social contribution, I think, "How does this help me right now?" If I can't get a reply, I refuse the bid, which makes room for more pressing matters on my calendar. Automate Repeat Tasks Automating some of these duties helped me streamline my work. For example, if you find yourself answering the same customer questions over and over again, your shop policies may need to be explained. Read Crunched for Time for more tips on handling repeat tasks? Put on Autopilot Routine Tasks.

Focusing on non-essential tasks can be tempting, rather than tackling more critical ones. If you have a negative emotional reaction to performing such activities, merely remembering your reaction will help. From there you can build tools or services to help you overcome the pull of procrastination. For starters, when I'm online, I get sidetracked easily so I stick to a simple routine that helps me stay off the Internet and on the right path. Keep your hand on the Award

Monitoring your progress is an important part of achieving the goals you and your business have set themselves. Getting a good picture of how far you have achieved your goals and what work still needs to be completed will give you the motivation you need to get through challenging times. When meeting your goals – or attaining smaller achievements along the way – note the difficult times and let yourself be appreciated. You did deserve it!

Now let us talk about creating a shop section on Etsy.

- Open the Shop Name page by clicking the Your Shop link at the top of any Etsy page, if it is not open already.
- Opens the Store Name tab.
- On the left-hand side of the page, click the Add Shop Sections button.
- The page opens to the Shop Areas.
- In the Build, a Section area enters a name for the new section.
- The name may have up to 24 characters in it.
- In addition to using the shop title and shop announcement, Google also uses your section titles as search keywords, opt for titles that double as likely keywords in the section.
- Click the button to Close.
- Etsy creates a section that uses the name you typed.
- Click the Create New Section button to add another segment, and repeat steps 3 and 4.
- Click the icon to the left of the section to adjust the order in which sections appear, and move it to the desired position in the order.

If you have not yet produced any shop listings, you will not be able to view parts on the main page of your store. But, once you create a list, — and allocate it to a section — the section will be displayed on the left side of your Etsy shop page.

Follow these steps to form a section:

- Go to the connection in your shop and go shopping name
- On the left-hand side of the page, click the Add Shop Sections button.
- In the Build, a Section area enters a name for the new section.
- The name may have up to 24 characters in it.
- In addition to using the shop title and shop announcement, Google also uses your section titles as search keywords. opt for titles that double as likely keywords in the section.
- Click the Save button and Etsy will use the name you typed to create a line.
- Click the Create New Section button to add another segment, and repeat steps 3 to 6.
- Click the icon to the left of the section to adjust the order in which sections appear, and move it to the desired position in the order.

Finally, rearrange. Go to the name of your store, and click. You will then see several options in a column along the left-hand side. Click "Options" to activate your shop's "Rearrange" feature.

CHAPTER TEN:

Marketing your Etsy store.

Marketing is a critical component of a successful business. Marketing is the total business activity system that determines the price, the promotion, and the distribution of wishes and needs, the services to a potential customer. Even if you make the most brilliant product ever invented on earth, if nobody knows about it, nobody will buy it. Successful marketing solves this issue by raising brand recognition and creating credibility. It, in effect, helps shoppers discover your products, creates faith and trust in customers, and contributes to sales and opportunities. When you mature Etsy Store's marketing strategy, you create a certain theory that will direct the company called the "Seven P Rule," which you will use to constantly review and reassess your business activities. These seven are commodity, size, promotion, location, packaging, positioning, and individuals. When goods, industries, consumers, and expectations evolve rapidly, you need to constantly update these seven PS to make sure you're on track and achieve the best potential results for you on the marketplace today.

User perspective

First of all, cultivate the practice of looking at your product as though you were an external marketing expert brought in to help the client determine whether or not it is in the right business at the moment. Ask crucial questions such as, "Is your existing product or service, or combination of goods and services, suitable and acceptable for today's market and customers?"

Whenever you have trouble selling as many of your goods or services as you would like, you need to cultivate the habit of objectively reviewing your company and ask, "Are these the best products or services for our customers today? Is there any product or service you sell now that you wouldn't bring out again now, knowing what you now know? Is your product or service superior to anything else available in some significant way as compared to your competitors? If so, then what is that? If not, might you be building a dominance area? In the current marketplace would you sell this product or service at all?

Tariffs and Plans

In a formula, the second P is the price. Build the practice of regularly updating and re-examining the prices of the goods and services you offer to ensure they are still relevant to current market realities. You sometimes have to lower your prices. At other times, heightening your prices may be sufficient. Many firms have discovered that the profitability of certain products or services does not justify the amount of effort and resources to produce them. They will lose a percentage of their customers by increasing their prices but the remaining percentage generates profit on each sale. Might this be nice for you?

Often you have to change the terms of sale and conditions. Often you can sell even more than you are now by extending the price over months or years and the interest you will receive would be more than compensating for the delay in cash receipts. Sometimes the products and services can be combined with special offers and special promotions. Often you can provide extra free products that cost you very little to manufacture but make your prices look much more appealing to your customers.

In business, as in nature, be open to revisiting that area whenever you experience resistance or frustration on any part of your sales or marketing plan. Be open to those possibilities perhaps the current pricing strategy for the current market is not suitable. Be open to the need to adjust the prices to stay competitive, survive, and prosper in a fast-changing environment where possible.

Advertising

The third practice in marketing and advertising is to still think in terms of the promotion. The promotion covers all the ways you tell your consumers about your goods or services, and also how you advertise them and sell them. Small changes in the way the goods are marketed and sold will result in drastic changes in the results. Only subtle improvements in your ads will lead to higher sales instantly. Experienced copywriters often can increase advertising response rates by actually changing the title of the commercial by 500 percent.

Large and small businesses in every sector are continuously experimenting with new ways to advertise, promote, and sell their goods and services. And here's the rule: Whatever marketing and sales tool you use today will stop working, sooner or later. Often for reasons you think it will stop working and sometimes for reasons you don't realize it will. In this case, the marketing and sales tactics will inevitably cease to work and you will have to find new approaches to sales, marketing and advertisement, deals, and strategies.

For any situation, the entrepreneur must make the correct choice about the very best place or location for the consumer to obtain important buying information about the product or service needed to make a purchase decision. Which is it with you? You should change it in what way? Where else do you sell services or products?

Place and Location

The fourth P in the marketing mix is where your product or service goes on sale. Establish the practice of evaluating and concentrating on the exact place where the salesperson meets the customer. A change in place can occasionally lead to a rapid increase in sales.

Your product can be sold in several different locations. Many companies use direct marketing, sending their salespeople out to meet and speak to the prospect directly. Many sell out via telemarketing. Some sell by catalog or by mail order. Others sell in retail establishments or at trade shows. Others offer other related goods or services in joint ventures. Some organizations use representatives of the suppliers or distributors. Most businesses use one or more of those strategies in combination.

Shipping, Packaging, and Delivery

The packaging is the fifth element inside the marketing mix. Build the habit of standing back and looking through the eyes of a vital prospect at any visual item in the packaging of your product or service. Remember, within the first 30 seconds of seeing you or any aspect of your business, people create their first impression about you. Simple changes in the product or service's packaging or exterior appearance can also lead to radically different consumer reactions.

About your company's packaging, product, or service, you should find all the consumer sees from the very first moment of interaction with your company. Into the procurement process. Packaging refers to the way that the product or service appears. Packaging also refers to your people and how they clothe and groom themselves. This refers to your offices, waiting rooms, brochures, correspondence, and every single visual element about your business. These all count. Nothing helps and everything hurts. Every is impacting the trust the customer has in dealing with you.

Position

Positioning for the next P. You will continually cultivate the habit of thinking about how you are placed within your customers' hearts and minds. How do people think about you and talk about you while you're out? How do people think about your business, and talk about it? In terms of the particular words people use when they identify you and your products to others, what place do you have in your market?

Steps to follow in your Etsy shop marketing

Identify the customer you want

You would need to recognize the person who is most likely to purchase from your store to start attracting potential customers to your small business. That is your main customer-the the person you will always remember when developing and promoting your product line. Knowing how and why your target customer makes a purchase will help you make educated decisions as you set up and scale up your business, and will eventually be crucial in deciding which marketing strategies can produce the most sales.

A demographic profile

If you're just starting, a rough description of your potential audience may be helpful. Picture the person who will be using your product. Is she the ideal host for a party? One proud owner of a pet? An aspirational green thumb? When you're designing products, find your core demographic distinguishing features. Factors such as age, level of income, local environment, cultural values, and personal preferences can all influence their purchasing habits.

Trace your statistics

As traffic and sales in your shop increase, statistics from your shop will start telling a tale about who your customers are. A subscription to Google Analytics will provide a breakdown of the demographics of your customers by age, location, gender, and interest. You can also search your Stats' Customers tab to learn stuff about how they shop, where they live and what kinds of products they are looking for. Are your clients looking for human wear too? When those search words tend to reappear, find those to be a key indicator of the lifestyle and interests of your target audience. What they're looking for will also give you some clues as to who your customers are shopping for.

Tap on fans and followers

Pay careful attention to what resonates with your fans as you collect views and Favorites on your Etsy listings. Your Stats Lists tab provides a simple view of which things perform best in terms of favorites and visits. When you feel like digging, you may also find out what your fans on Etsy are favoriting somewhere else.

In the same way, your social feeds can provide valuable insights about your customers. If you're using Facebook, Instagram, telegram, or another social platform to communicate with your audience, the tastes, habits, and taste preferences of each new follower will help you paint a composite image of your target client. Set aside time to press and learn more about their lifestyles and activities. And don't stop engaging with each other. For example, encouraging your followers on Facebook to tag you in pictures where they use your products can give you a clear understanding of how your brand blends into their daily lives.

Take part in related societies and fora

By engaging in online groups and forums where your customers already connect, learn more about your target market. Join the conversation and ask lots of questions; you may be able to identify popular patterns and points of pain that will help you refine your product selection. If a recurrent discontent among millennials, for example, if a recurrent millennial annoyance is that they cannot find jeans with pockets that are big enough to accommodate their mobile phones, you can attach oversized pockets to your denim collection. It also means that when choosing the marketing keywords wide pockets will be a significant feature to highlight.

Check the tags on your label

Experimenting with demographic-specific tags can be a perfect way to gain concrete insights into what and what does not resonate with shoppers. For example, if you tag your product with "birthday present" or "dad's gift" and see a traffic boost, you may also think about providing gift wrap and using more holiday tags to cater to your customers. Try adding tags that represent your assumed target audience's styles and tastes. Keywords emulating motifs, patterns, colors, and the item's general spirit can work wonderfully. Get familiar with the lingo that your audience would most likely use in your names, explanations, and tags and reproduce those words.

Understand your consumer competition

Your work essentially helps to create an identity for your target customers, using concrete specifics to bring them to life. Take the time to get to know these hypothetical shoppers. Offer them a name and background in education, and occupation, and family history. Bear in mind their desires and expectations as you fine-tune your product line and devise your marketing plan. Tell yourself, which kind of message resonates best? An inspirational Facebook message at breakfast for a busy mum? A product funded on a high-end web blog Sunday? Now that you've identified who your target customers are, you can determine where, when, and how to most effectively engage with them during their purchaser journey.

Finding the brand identity and delivering an exhibition specially

Your target clients will need a compelling reason to select your product over any other product on the market. And how do you see to it that your shop stands out from the competition? The secret to this is to have a clear brand name. You will learn how to create a successful brand in the following section, by setting specific goals for your company and consistently delivering on them.

A Logo speaks Promise

A logo is a promise an organization makes to its customers. Not only is your brand identity the picture that your company presents, but it is also the collection of standards that your clients associate with that picture. A good brand shows to your customers what your company stands for and what your goods experience will deliver

Marque ambassadors

That one can be daunting for new Etsy shop— and if you're just starting, it's very hard to know how to do it — people just don't talk much about it. So, to use it is an AWESOME device, since you are hiring an advertising agency, just for a fraction of the size.

Brand ambassadors are people you send free products on their blog and social media pages in return for them endorsing your brand + goods. There's another word floating around—"brand lovers "that's close, except you don't have to give your product away for free. Usually, you offer a discount code (A MAJOR ONE— like 50 percent off) + have a minimum buying requirement per those people endorse every quarter and then in the same way that brand ambassadors do.

There are advantages + disadvantages for both, brand ambassadors are better because they tend to push your products a bit more frequently, simply because they get your product free and feel obliged to make it worth your time so you keep it on.

Any method is great though (especially if you are in the human wear business) it's a fairly easy way to get in front of large audiences with very little effort on your part— you just have to submit the product.

And how do you find those guys? One of the easiest ways to find the first brand ambassadors is to launch social media with a shout-out. The people there who follow you? These guys are already some of your biggest fans and in return for advertising, a lot of them will love free stuff.

I made many call-outs only on my Instagram, and every time I got hundreds of answers.

Type overlap

Ready to touch THOUSANDS of people with your product? It is one of the go-to(s) of my very favorite ads because it's so sticky, free. Yet unbelievably simple. Your first may take a few hours (just to get the hang of it) but then? You are the pro here always act like it. Here is a list of basics:
- Start by choosing some of the items you want to sell.

- Use the item to create a "theme" you want to concentrate on
- Find goods that suit your theme from other Etsy / e-commerce sites (note: it is CRITICAL to make sure they are NOT too close to a product-they should be complementary and not competitive)
- Start to hang out where your audience is
- The audience will trigger you more about your product in an environment where you are welcomed. That's cool if you're there to socialize. But if you're hanging out to try to get more views + sales to your shop in the Etsy forums, you're wasting your precious time
- Think of where the target audience is sitting — will they read any magazines? Were they online fora members? Do they waste their time on Facebook? Don't you even know where they were spending their time? Then ask them about it! You need to find out where they hang out, so you need to start HANGING OUT WITH THEM.
- It's great to hang out with other shop owners to build up business relationships and get vague advice, but if you want to make more sales (and I guess you're probably doing that), then you're spending your time in the wrong place.
- The goal here is to show up as a friendly resource + expert in the interests of your target market. A case in point? If you're selling trendy female jewelry, you'll want to start posting on style-blogger articles or joining fashion magazine forums. Nonetheless, you won't want to hang out on jewelry-making blogs, because the only socializing you'll get would be with other jewelry-makers — and they'll not buy their items.
- Note — you don't just want to put your shop out there — give genuine suggestions or solutions to any ongoing conversations, and ALWAYS provide a link back to your blog/shop where they will find more examples. Give, and offer, and then ask.

For getting your product out there, social media sites are awesome, but the one thing that sucks about them? You never have full power over them. Take for example what Instagram did by updating the newsfeed algorithm earlier this year. Everywhere, small shop owners went mentally because suddenly their product wasn't going to appear in everybody's stream. And what do you know? There's nothing else that we can do.

Take a marketing list. If you have no mailing list yet, then it's time to change that. Mailing lists sound so old-fashioned, but I'm here to tell you there's a reason everybody's promoting them — they're the only marketing tool you're in charge of.

Instagram, Twitter, Facebook, and all other social media competitions are a dime a million, but very fairly so! They can be unbelievably successful in bringing the brand in an incredibly short period, in front of more people. But the trick? Make the most of your competitions so you don't waste precious time or your purchase. Here are some tips to get the most out of your social gift account:

• Make it easy to enter your customers are busy and have no time to write a 500-word essay about why your products are so amazing. Simple entries to tag a friend or repost your photo on their account

• Up the ante if you're getting a positive response to the contest, but not the answer you've been waiting for, then raise your prize. Such suggestions can be to make the grand prize larger, have several runner-up prizes, or to include different ways in which people can join.

• Advertise it more than once Please do NOT just post about your contest once if you do something else, and then presume that everybody is going to see the post and join. They will not. While we believe that people are on social media all the time, it is possible that about 75% of your audience will not see your post the first time. And that is perfect! And this is why it will start to bring at a later time on that day and the next few days new subscribers

• Offer a consolation prize everyone who entered your gift wanted a chance to win, but since the overwhelming majority of the entrants won't win the contest, they offer a discount code to follow up on the winner's announcement. You know they weren't winning, but you still appreciate they've been proactive and entered your contest, and you're rewarding them for it. Plus, they 're already worked up as a "warm" audience because they've already shown a) interest, and b) most likely envisioned themselves as the winner, and imagined what it's like to own the award.

Influencer/blogger social media pitch

Just how many people have blogs / social media pages for the sole purpose of selling the goods of others, will shock you. Although I would suggest reaching out to anyone and anyone you think will suit your brand well (and just as importantly — would have an audience that suits your brand well), look for bloggers/influencers who have their email on their social media handle. These are the types of people you want to work with — they are used to pitch and understand how your product can be marketed.

One thing I always suggest is that you have a short email contract as part of your agreement — I've seen it happen time and again (to me, too) that people would send out stuff to influencers and then never hear from them again. Don't allow that to happen! A simple, casual email agreement is the BEST way to ensure that everyone holds their deal to a close.

Word of Mouth

Word of mouth is certainly one of Etsy's most effective forms of marketing for small retailers. But implementing it is challenging too, especially if your budget is limited. You need to consciously enable them to exchange knowledge about you to create more business from your current customers and you need to have an opportunity for people to persuade their mates to make a purchase.

The best approach to do that is to:

• Begin a referral system giving discounts to customers getting you more.

• Begin a campaign giving a discount to your loyal customer and friend they bring with you.

• Launch competitions that promote social media sharing of your ads with a randomly chosen winner's prize.

• Provide positive reviews to any customer who discusses your shop at their blogs.

• Invite loyal clients to serve as brand ambassadors.

Marketing by Email

Etsy shop owners frequently make the mistake of ignoring email newsletters as a means of reaching out to their customers. Nonetheless, as this email advertising guide for online retailers illustrates, email marketing provides the highest ROI about SEO, keyword ads, banner ads, and web displays. Therefore, it can be a huge boon for your business to invest in email marketing software and content to fill your newsletters with.

The guide can teach you how to set up a proper campaign for email marketing. Nevertheless, by using this method Etsy retailers have an extra challenge. The challenge is the generation of content because you not only need to provide updates on new items and sales in your store. For E-Mail to be successful in marketing, you must fill in your emails with useful material, such as how-to guides, simple DIY tutorials, suggestions about how to best use your goods, and so on. Such emails must be regular (1-3 daily) and flexible.

Allies with other retailers

Etsy Teams is an excellent service that helps retailers connect and share tips on how to market their shops. For successful marketing in 2019, however, you don't even need to use your peers' mutual information.

You will also be liaising with other vendors selling goods that complement yours. Notice that you need to reach out to those who would benefit from matching your goods with their own, not rivals. Then, start a campaign offering special combined product kits. This will provide you with access to the audiences of your new partners, and through your reach.

Optimization of Etsy search

You can never forget that you need to configure it explicitly for Etsy Search to improve your shop's chances of being found. This kind of render optimization is not the same as normal Google Search SEO.

Persevere

If you had to be offered one word to succeed in running a small company or a shop on Etsy, then a determination will have to be! Do I feel good? Yes, I do this year! When you know you have a great product with good prices, you can learn online selling semiconducting as you go – just keep going. Don't yield! Be ready to succeed and you'll be successful! Now go, do, give you good luck!

Seek to be as a pro in every area of your job as possible

Your Etsy store could also look like a reputable business, and feel like it. Buyer's online need to have credibility. That means good branding, good images, fast delivery, prompt, courteous answers to the questions and a product of quality. Having been featured on Etsy finds a couple of times early on I found a lot of my sales are by word of mouth. If you want to rave about your goods for customers, then customer service is all. Two friends are telling 2 people, tell 2 acquaintances and then you have a large customer base. Yeah, and be yourself, just enjoy what you're doing and build a need for good people! It's the smallest important information!

Photos are what you market your product

On Etsy a lot goes into good selling: staying busy, forming teams, making unique products, pricing, accepting the changes, fast delivery, excellent customer service, the list seems endless! Yet all these efforts are in vain if your driving traffic gets to your shop and you find images that don't captivate the buyer. Pictures that sell your goods by making a personality unique to every object and everything that is its own. Pictures IS what they offer. Natural lighting and great close-ups, wherever possible, go a long way toward helping an inanimate object something a buyer is curious about and wants to know more about

Finding a seat is extremely important

Which is your wish you couldn't seem to be working out there? Anything else should be done, or otherwise? I started making Moon pads because I wanted prettier, more affordable menstrual pads. I started my other Etsy business because I couldn't find pearl snaps on Moon pads and hoped other people would also like them. And then, there they are. Images, videos and photos! All right, pictures' a must. The month I got Photoshop, my sales went up rapidly and dramatically.

Being Special

The greatest piece of advice is being one of a kind. Let your imagination thrive, and make your work stand out. Try for something different that's special to you. I feel like shoppers enjoy this variety.

It brings sales to create something unique. We love being special and want something that can simultaneously reflect the distinction. Not only does the individuality make your shop stand out from the others, but it also makes your shop fascinating too. Everybody has their taste, and they purchase unique products as a response. So try to be special!

Offer better customer service

It may sound like this is a cliché tip but I've turned dissatisfied customers into loyal buyers by keeping that in mind. I stick to my pledge 'Enjoy it' if a client doesn't like it or something doesn't work for them (if they don't like it, they get back their money). I do whatever I can to correct any problems with the orders promptly and kindly. I lost a package in the mail 2 times in a row to a foreign buyer. I reimbursed her money after the second time, and sent out a third one that made it for her. She was so grateful for the service, and left her reviews saying it was her best customer service ever. Often, she buys out of my shop. Consumers really enjoy it when a seller treats them well. They share these experiences, and almost always return. This not only builds a great character for your company but it also keeps customers coming back and back.

Quantity: You can't expect someone to spend time in your store if you don't have anything to offer. Just a few things in your store, or even 30 things, don't offer the customer a range of choices. It wasn't until we had 50 things in our store that we began selling consistently and we know we've got to have at least 100 items in the store to do well on Etsy. End-of-year holiday planning target is 200+ items that we will begin production in June.

Quality: It is tough to create an incredible handmade product. Etsy lets you show off quality in a variety of ways: great photos of the depths of your work, ratings, and the shop's new About tab. Nevertheless, one of the best ways for your customers to learn more about your products is through a blog, where you could not only highlight custom orders but also discuss the creative process. This could earn a little more love for your business and get you, clients.

Give excellent customer service

It is important to provide the best service possible to the customers from the first to the last point of contact. After six years of service, the majority of my clients are returning customers and/or referrals from past clients. I give exceptional service, besides making an outstanding product. Communication is a central component of my services decision. I make sure, upon receipt, that I accept each order and send daily updates on the status of the order, including tracking information while shipping. My customers let me know they appreciate my excellent customer service and I believe this has played a key role in my success.

Review Deal

When possible, always give the consumer a chance to try out your items before they decide to invest in a full-size piece. If you're producing items that can't be sold as samples – have something inexpensive in your shop that won't cost much but will be an opportunity to experience touch, and give the idea of what you are doing. It can be a tiny key chain, a handkerchief, something that demonstrates your craftsmanship and efficiency. Even, if you can- add with every order anything for free. Just the smallest thing can be a great nice surprise and will make the customer feel happy.

It takes money to make a living

I still have the best luck with blogs that I enjoy reading while searching for blogs to advertise your goods with. I believe it goes hand in hand with ensuring you know your target market. Just knowing which kind of person will buy your goods. Will that person probably have read the same blog? I reinvested my profit back into advertising within the first 6 months. Letting go of the money wasn't always easy, but it certainly paid off, and helped me get a good start!

Promote, build, nurture

It's easy to advertise just about everything in the Internet age ... including your new handcrafted piece. Facebook and Twitter are great marketing resources but find forums that fit your customers to sell your product to your niche. Other "private" networks are sprouting up all the time. Etsy forums are a perfect way for more popular sellers to find motivation and feedback to help make you the best you can be. Today, word-of-mouth is the most powerful source of publicity. So, provide business cards with any order, or ask the local coffee shop, restaurant, etc. if you can display your cards for others to distribute and turn around and share. So, build when you aren't promoting! Get the crafting to stay new and ahead of the curve on the next big concept! Good customer support: Customer care goes beyond and beyond. Customers shop where gratitude is felt. Excellent goods combined with excellent customer service offer loyal customers who chat about your shop to their peers.

There are no new clients

I read once to do business somewhere as if you could never find another new client ... the only hope of success was to turn current customers into loyal customers. It's a bit of a tongue-in-cheek, but I often think of it. What do my current customers want to cherish? How can I fill out an order and connect with someone (either online or in-person) in a manner that makes them fondly remember us and want to come back? This helps me slow down at shows and even during busy periods when I fill in orders — double-checking the contents, packaging, and thank-you note. I never seek to fill out an order with an incomplete product, even one whose labors Label is somewhat off-center, so when they meet us at shows or give us a message, they seek to listen to us, taking a moment for a respectful interchange.

Get in touch & make friends

Offer codes for specials, discounts, & coupons. It's a smart way to bring in new customers and also to reward loyal customers.

Virtually Tangible

Build an online summary of your product which is the next best tangible thing. It includes a concise representation of your product from various perspectives and views in the catalog and plain, uncluttered photographs of your item. Better atmospheric pictures too! Potential customers can't pick up your items for scrutiny so offer them time to examine your objects, so give them the next best thing ... I like to call it "virtual tangibility."

Integrity matters

My popularity at Etsy depends not only on what I have to sell but also on the range of cosmetics. I offer products I wasn't able to find in the marketplace as a consumer so I made them myself. I listen to what my customers are looking for and sell those items afterward. Without flooding my customers with too many details I want all my cosmetics to surpass expectations. Pictures and explanations should be reliable and when selling cosmetics online it's very necessary to be available to answer questions.

Branding and Consumers Repeat

I had given a lot of thought to building a brand before I hand stitched my first fabric. I decided to incorporate my goal into a recognizable and meaningful name. Next, I had the label labeled, and the birth of A Helping Hand Bag. I've worked hard to make my store look unified but it's my logo that's my strongest marketing and builds name recognition and returns customers as a result. With Etsy that and that competition, I feel it's important to have a high-quality product, great customer service, and a brand that my customers will recognize.

Your picture tells you something

Will your pictures draw clients or do you get overlooked? I have done a lot of surfing since I first started on Etsy. I thought I wanted to see how they got there if somebody was already good. I looked at the front page and checked the pictures carefully to see where or how I could develop my own. You need to think like a customer, choose any category and browse and click to do so. What is it that makes you click? Several customers told me my photographs were what attracted them into my shop and hopefully, my explanations and customer service kept them there.

Write the Job

Tell the story behind your job or motivation. I know I am more fascinated by a product containing a paragraph with creative process detail. For me, this is a challenge because I often find it difficult to express precisely what through drawing or painting meant but I seek to describe myself as honestly as possible. I typically express myself with laughter, because in both my drawing and writing, that's what comes naturally to me. Hopefully sharing your thoughts and processes will allow your audience to relate to you and your work, and feel more connected.

Do customized research, quick shipping & communication

For me.... sales went up when I began doing people's personalized jobs. People enjoy being imaginative and making something special

& their own. Everyone always keeps saying that they like how I get my products out to them quickly and they don't have to wait long as other sellers do. When someone orders something they already think about using it and they're excited to try it out! They also really appreciate my communication on thanking them when the order will be filled out, and when it's sent with confirmation.

Performance

A good brand lets potential buyers keep their shop fresh in mind. When we started it was as easy as creating a simple theme to tie up with our avatar in our Etsy banner. Earlier, we also integrated the theme into our business cards, Facebook, Twitter, etc... One of Etsy's many amazing things is that they give you plenty of chances to share the story of your exclusive handmade pieces! Spend time thinking about what best reflects the things you market to customers, and create something coherent and memorable.

Stick to it

Never surrender. Everything is possible. It is undoubtedly true that when one door closes another one opens, but only if you think a good door is opened and just let it happen. If something doesn't work, then find out how something can be modified so it does. You have to live and breathe whatever your passion is.

Find out what fits best for you

I believe the thing that's contributing to my biggest success in my Etsy store is playing with items before I've found the best ones for me and my business. I used to make a range of bags and accessories, introducing new designs and fabrics as well as removing those that didn't sell. In time I learned to predict what a good seller will be and how to increase the sales of that item with a wide range of fabrics. (Bonus tip: gray wool does not go out of style!)

Keep things new in your shop

Add a new product, take pictures on older ones, add new lines of goods and redesign packaging. It's the best time to refresh it when your shop is slow so it still looks fresh and exciting for your customers.

Find a niche market and render products in markets that are not readily available

Our company started because my mom wanted a microwave heating pad for her neck and shoulders and we couldn't find a suitable one in stores-so I created one. From there we developed our company around producing innovative items for hot and cold therapy packaging. Some of our best-sellers initially started telling a customer "can you do this?"

I love to make handcrafted goods. Since I love using artisanal goods! I will retreat into my innermost selfish being when I'm in a creative slump and think ... What can I create as a treat for myself? If I'm fortunate it typically gives rise to a spark that drives me to wild exploration, resulting in new scents and soaps. If my ideas sell, awesome! If not, I've got a fresh soap, perfume, or candle bar that I'm going to enjoy while mulling about potential ideas. I urge everyone to be true to themselves, to build that which they love, to live their passions, and to be directed from their hearts.

Love the Shop

If you enjoy what you're doing and do the best you can to make your things and shop the best you can, your future customers are going to pick up on that and want to be apart from the beautiful thing that you made. Be open to suggestions, and be not afraid of experimentation.

Impossible is ideal

I see so many starting entrepreneurs assume that once they get their pictures right or have their SEO in place, it's all going to be perfect and sales just start rolling in. This is an utter fallacy. Why? For what? Since you are never going to get better and your shop is never going to be fine. There's SO much you can do to improve your company.

Keep it personalized

As an Etsy shop, I seek to offer a special handmade experience to every buyer. This means that every order that goes out is wrapped and packed like a birthday present: gift wrap, tissues, ribbon, a personalized note, and even a unique decorated envelope. Each item needs to feel intimate, not something that came out of an order on the production line. Put in the time to deliver the highest quality product. I have lots of repeat customers who leave reviews on how good my bags are made.

Put in the time .... to take the best pictures you can manage and edit.

Put in the time .... to regularly list items (use all tags!)

Put in the time....to inspire. I'm using Instagram, Facebook, and Whatsapp and promotional. Promotion of research/advertising/blogs which reach your target market.

Put the time in....to respond promptly to customer requests or conversations. Love good service to customers!

Take Fantastic Pictures

A photo is worth a thousand words. Product pictures are the best they can be, without being able to pick up and feel the objects. So, the product photography is high up on my list when it comes to my Etsy Company, right next to product quality. I use a white backdrop almost always because there are no distractions from the items. I use natural lighting, I get the best morning lighting, even though not too heavy. I just brighten up the context when it comes to picture editing in comparison to displaying the specifics of the fabric, crop the picture so that the product is in the middle and it's finished.

Persevere

Since I've been selling on Etsy since 2007, one thing I can say for sure is that a lot of shops will come and go but, in my view, perseverance is what has made mine popular. One of my favorite quotes in my shop profile is: "Progress seems to be mostly a matter of holding on when others have let go." In the online handmade industry, you cannot possibly have any form of success unless you can stick with it and keep up with current trends. And it's just been convenient for me to keep going because I enjoy what I do. Your art loves No matter what it is, just persevere.

Update

Create new and affordable items for my customers as much as possible. New goods are revitalizing sales. Much of the time I've had that experience when I launch new pieces, whether they're jewelry, fabric prints, wood prints, etc. They allow you to increase sales to existing customers, but also attract other customers and eventually sell more of all your goods, not just the one you launch.

Inventing the store once again

Whether it's starting from scratch or starting from the top, the trick is to constantly track what's happening on Etsy. What colors are in? What is it that supports Etsy? What is sold in season? What kinds of animals, forms, and natural elements appear on the front page? I relate my findings to what I could create. I just sew. What you make can affect your style. Make stuff that you enjoy and others would probably enjoy too (if not seek another angle).

Trial and Mistake

Etsy is a perfect place for sharing and using the "trial and error" approach to see what is going to appeal to others. I wanted to set up a shop where I could sell nature and art using my handbags. Canvas-Canvas. I learned soon that the shape of the purse and the materials used were just as critical as the design put on the pocket. Through continuously working on my projects and seeing the amount of "views" they got, it helped me realize what had to improve and what worked.

Search for Expert Act

You have to see what you do with yourself. This includes filling out all Etsy deals such as Shop Announcement / Profile, About Page and Policy List, a Shop Banner, and a full row of Featured Products. Shops that skip these tell me that no one cares about the store. Be sure to include information such as size and feature in your summary. Just saying here is a pretty candle that I made without giving size and burning time with pictures of the actual item sends me running for the hills. Saying something like I am not liable in your scheme if an element ship makes me run the other way too. You, as a retailer, are also liable until the customer receives his item and is happy with it. My shop runs according to the Golden Standard, treat each customer wishes to be handled as you would. It's how I developed a loyal customer base that returns year after year irrespective of what Etsy shifts.

Be known for delivering excellent customer support and going above and beyond for your customers! That's a big part of my performance. Build the name for yourself, have a product that customers want, and reply as quickly as possible to inquiries/emails. Whether your customer has a specific request, needs something fully personalized, or is searching for details, they will appreciate that you are timely and courteous in your answers and will recommend you to their friends and family.

Packaging puts us into a complete circle

I found that you have to love, like, or at least accept all facets of what you are doing, or that motivating yourself to work is very hard. I enjoy the more boring parts of what I do in the sweatshop – packing, stitching on clothes and bags labels, casting, printing, email response, shipping details, etc. Such things take longer than you'd expect, but I think it shows in the finished product that the consumer will tell you how much time and energy you invested in making it all that way. Packaging things well and thoughtfully is extremely necessary. Also, it is always nice to have an unexpected goodie in the box, as it makes it available and more fun than that, which can lead to repeat sales.

Dedication and hard work

All the time, I get asked how I run a profitable Etsy shop. My best response is a lot of hard work and commitment to doing what you enjoy. Work is enjoyable for me and I learned a lot along the way. I started with two things that I loved to do, sewing and designing and it took off. I've put a lot of hard work in many ways of improving my shop. Use Facebook to chat with customers to give them a glimpse into my life to aim for an outstanding product, customer service and the best images I can manage.

Recognize their order and Make it FAST

Everybody needs immediate gratification, particularly when they make a purchase online. If you don't already have one, invest in a postal scale, bubble wrap, poly mailers, packing peanuts and boxes .... whatever you need for shipping. When possible purchase in bulk and don't forget to sign up with your local freecycle.com group to chase free shipping supplies too. Mailing labels can also be bought (again eBay, super cheap) or labels can be printed on plain paper and tape to packaging.

I think most of my sales are created by my item descriptions (something that made moving to wholesale challenging for me) that usually includes a snippet about my inspiration for every perfume. I get a lot of answers about my writing, and those conversations fostered some great friendships that turned into my best repeat customers (who gave great referrals) too. I'd say something you enjoy is important to do and let your interest come through. On Etsy, in particular, everyone is happy to be involved in the handmade economy, they want to vote for great shops and if they feel interested, they will do so much of the marketing for you. Etsy is all about culture, it goes a very long way to be nice and connect with customers.

CHAPTER 11:

Powerful branding techniques and tactics.

Over the past eight years, Etsy has taken the world of small business by storm, combining online retail with an art show / antique shop feel. Some people have chosen to sell on Etsy because they love making stuff and showcasing it or they like "flipping" older pieces, showing their style and how they can be combined with new or different stuff to make trendy alternatives to off the shelf products. Etsy provides a fairly cheap way of entering this market, without the seasonal or regional constraints of trade fairs or Perhaps retail room leasing and staffing costs.

Customers love shopping at Etsy because they want something handmade and carefully produced, and enjoy knowing it was planned or crafted by a real person. It's not for cheapskates – the real skinflints browse the thrifts in search of legitimate bargains and deep rebates. Etsy is an experience of being treated by a person to a specific item made or found exclusively for you. It strongly appeals to millions of people growing up on mass-manufactured, relentlessly selling everything. Just as bread tastes fresher at a farmer's market, soap bought from an Etsy storefront seems more authentic. You can't make genuine mass-produce knowing this, how do you, as an Etsy storefront owner, brand yourself in a way that does not compromise what Etsy customers find to be an essential part of the transaction-the reality?

We live in a highly competitive environment and if they want to make their business successful, it is in the interest of any organization to develop real relationships with its customer. Helpful advice is to start operating on an advantage or a competitive edge. Knowing all facets of the brand of your competitor will help you decide what actions to take to attract clients, by leveraging the weak points of your competitor.

Developing a plan that illustrates the competition's positive and poor options should give you a stronger perspective on what course of action suits your company best. Every day the majority of people face thousands of brand choices when shopping for products.

Yet the same people often want a trust-based product. Do I know this business, like, And trust? Do I know what sells the company? Have I ever tried them before? Is the new product going to meet my needs? They are all legitimate questions that consumers ask themselves every day when they contemplate purchasing from you.

Even though regular brands offer the same quality product as other brands, the big names have one advantage, the complete trust of their customers. This is why it is important to create a strong bond with your client that separates you from another brand.

Branding is about communicating the ideals of your company, and the right strategies can and will help your business grow. It's no wonder brands have become a reliable commodity, it's called brand equity because it has a meaning, given that if you hit the top-of-mind of the consumers, the revenue is not reliant on the product itself. They already know they like you and your company and trust you. (And they'll express the confidence as a word of mouth to others).

Implementing a label strategy has been shown to improve the reputation of the company of every product or service. Any successful branding strategy wins the confidence of the consumer, and what's more important, it continues to expand.

One big step towards financial stability is understanding which approaches work and which ones do not. The mission statement of most businesses is packed with far-fetched expectations and unachievable targets, making it impossible for the company to take off. Dismantle the purpose of the organization, and give it a reasonable structure and planning. The distinction between a failed business and a good business can be identified by splitting the task into different objectives.

Identify the needs of the target group after the mission statement provides a straightforward direction to each of the goals set. A useful tip is to test, with the same customer, what the customer wants they must have. Every good product marketing campaign requires not only a strong demand but also a fundamental need. Hence, get to know what the customer wants, and play by adding an enticing element for that target market accordingly.

You must first understand what branding is. A brand is not just a mark, as it once was when it appeared on cattle's backsides. Yes, you need a logo-an image that identifies your business and makes its products recognizable immediately. Yet you need more than that – you need to define what you are and what makes your goods special and important in the minds of your consumers and, most desirable, the general public.

Phase one will then be to go ahead and identify what you are and what makes your goods special and important for you. Just ponder what you've got to sell, and how your stuff is different from everybody else. Using your friends and family as sounding boards and seek to get suggestions that will help. When you have that down, then tackle the logo.

When designing your logo, choose one that reflects who you are in a way that appeals to your target market in particular. Choose carefully regarding color and design. If you want to invoke Grandma's kitchen of yesteryear with your shop, the best option is probably not black and white. See if you can find someone with graphic design knowledge – A professional marketing firm, an accomplished friend or even an acquaintance with whom you can trade skills for the product.

Infographics: Extend the Language

What better way to develop your brand by taking your content to the public? Either facts, stats, or even infographics of the learning process has always been a great tool for sharing the powerhouse content with appealing data. An infographic's strength is that it causes people to share information with peers so that it appears useful to them. Share exciting subject in the form of infographics, as visitors come to your blog. This is where designers and authors work together to create a visitor-engaging post that can be quickly shared on sites for social media. You are not only going to provide your guests with interesting facts and statistics, but you are also encouraging them to be gracious enough to spread the word. This will eventually move your brand from one channel to another as your consumers spread the word, but the tool that will help your content transfer matters a lot is social media, so never underestimate it. Despite the thousands of posts available online, try to keep a list of your audience's interest.

Update 3D technic

3-D photography tops the list of best branding strategies to be used by companies in 2019. Technology has a major impact on branding. When you unveil brand new and state-of-the-art visuals, people will continue to raise their standards and expect leading brands to meet that quality.

That is what we see in the branding strategies for 3D imagery. Companies use innovative modeling tools to integrate spectacular and photo-realistic 3D images into their marketing activities. It blurs the line between visuals created by computers and those produced in real life.

The 3D branding technique uses acute eye and jaw-dropping visuals for information while producing photographs whose primary aim is to give onlookers a 'wow' experience.

Complex Details

Intricate decorative features are gaining considerable popularity in the modern bus world. It includes giving more personality to your brand by adding more flora and embellishments.

It draws its influence from the styles of art deco and baroque architecture. It also gets inspiration for the popularity of hand-drawn illustrations in modern days. Specific ornamental features that minimalist tend to strip away typify the technique.

Many of the telltale features include, among others, visual flourishes to fill negative space, parallel and focus lines, and subtle details such as individual feathers, wrinkles, and eyelashes. The branding technique also has repeated patterns of ornate and interlocking shapes.

While this trend is creating some of the most artistic and beautiful images for any company, the shape-lifting technique should not be overlooked. It will make sure you have a pared-down version.

Often, visual information goes a long way to improve you. But in some areas, you will still need simpler stuff. Among the branding strategies you shouldn't leave behind in 2020 is detailed detail, generally speaking.

What's a tag on it?

A number! Your name conveys a significant part of the brand identity from the get-go. It'll be anywhere, everywhere, everywhere in your social network, every post, every package you send out! And you'd like to make sure you're careful about it. Your name is the beginning of the story that you tell your customers, and as with any piece of your brand, you want it to flow and show the special and authentic experience that you are offering.

Do whatever you think. Your name is your oath. This might sound like common sense, but how many times did you feel let down by a corporation or seller who didn't bring the sale to a halt? Yeah, life happens sometimes and you may have to fall back and punt. Yet if that's the case, express your way through it out! The last thing you want is that the image of your company is one of over-promising and under-delivery. Branding is the business personality, it's the human aspect that allows customers and potential customers to interact with you, so just like humans, being a good communicator is important!

Post content and offer interest regularly

What value are you bringing to the table? Sharing new information? Your value proposition is entertainment? Are you a marketing and sales think tank leader? If you want your brand to expand, you have to walk around and share knowledge with you Your Expertise Field.

Because of authenticity, relatability, and credibility people are drawn to personal brands. If you're not enthusiastic about what you're doing, conceiving it as an authentic material would be hard for it. If you do not use the right social media, you're not going to appeal to the right audiences. If you can't offer real value, your brand just won't get exposure.

Creating a Group

Personal brands will not have the same quality of potential to develop and thrive without committed followers and partners involved.

Consistency is paramount

We'll also see an Etsy store that destroys it with beautiful product images! But instead, a banner or emblem would miss the same store. Or maybe they have a fantastic shop sign, a simple logo, but then their explanations don't match the tone of the branding. Let's be clear. When you present your brand as optimistic and a little bit cheeky, then make sure all the branding parts match. Logo, banner, product picture, copy everything. You want to match each of those pieces individually. Again, it's important that your past and potential customers connect every step of the way with you and don't get confused by different messages.

Talking of shop banners and logos... It is probably the field where we have the most potential for overall development. There are so many amazing artists and creators on the Etsy platform and they're so passionate about what they're doing! But sometimes, since they are busy designing and producing, they struggle to express that enthusiasm to their clients. The face of your company is a strong emblem and a shop banner. It's an easy way to interact with your niche aesthetically, upfront.

You don't have to lay down thousands of dollars to make a decent logo. Some companies and designers are running the gambit. Do your work, build a branding budget, and continue from there. It's easier to have anything than nothing. If you need to start tiny, then that's all right! The important thing is that from the get-go you have a logo and shop banner that is cohesive and that is part of your branding strategy.

Relationships matter

So much for marketing and advertising, these days is about establishing relationships! As e-commerce is on the rise, we are increasingly inclined to take advice from those we know about goods and transactions and not from conventional types of advertisement. This will certainly be part of your brand building real relationships with your customers. Don't just sell out, make a friend! Customers come and go but there's always culture! So, make one.

Build an email list, stay in touch, let people in, give them a look at your working day behind the scenes, and get them involved in the things you're passionate about. It doesn't matter how amazing the goods are, at the end of the day. If you don't work to cultivate relationships and create community, you'll probably consider stability and survival to be tougher fighting.

Employee Commitment

Achieving a sense of consistency is crucial if you want to create brand awareness, as we have discussed before. And while a style guide will help you create a consistent digital experience, it is equally important to know how your employees can interact with consumers and reflect the brand.

If your brand is fun and bubbly via Twitter commitments, then it wouldn't make sense if a customer called in and had a grumpy, monotonous representative linked, right?

Fidelity

When you have people already who love you, your business, and your brand, don't just sit there. Pay them back for love. These customers have gone out their way to write about you, tell their friends about you, and act as ambassadors for your brand. Early cultivation of loyalty from these people will yield more returning customers — and greater profit for your company.

Give them credit!

It doesn't matter whether you come onto the market as a low-cost rival, a luxury supplier, or a combination of the two. Whatever you do, behave well. Provide goods which are what you claim they are and bring value to the lives of your customers! If you're building a brand that's rocking, but selling a product that isn't, then it was all for nothing.

Any of the world's logos, brand names, and good communication won't make up for a shop that isn't fundamentally placed to offer their customers interest. What matters is that you find a way to communicate and have a service, experience, or product that brightens the day of whoever does business with you, doesn't matter what you do.

Tap 'Natural Genius' into your Business

Ignite the spark of creativity which triggers and uncovers the brand or company's collective native genius. This will encourage a diverse attitude towards forward-thinking innovations or ideas that form the organization's fabric. Allow this bottom-up approach from all team members to explain how the whole is described and thus reflected in the brand, by these individual elements. To boost your sales shape your brand culture.

Pursue opportunities for public speaking

Professional opportunities for public speaking are a perfect opportunity for an individual to be a corporate brand advocate, be seen as a subject matter expert, and elevate their brand. In addition to this concept, a corporation should exploit the personal identity of an employee to enhance the corporate image of the organization.

Set your expertise and focus on that

Make sure you first establish your level of expertise when establishing or expanding your brand, which often requires that you become more focused on your activities. When the customer is aware of your specific business interest, it is easier to then use your imagination to decide which practices are best for your brand expansion.

Think in the scope of experience

Ask: How does it work for you? What is your product like? What terms are people using to identify you? Your personal and professional brand comes from people's experience and what's being said about you when you leave the house. Authenticity, accessibility, a strong experience, and close connections allow you to stand out.

Collaborate to create material for Videos

One of the people's biggest fears is waking up in front of a camera. It doesn't scream narcissism to let your organization know you want to help expand its brand, engage in video, and be interviewed on internal or external media. It is also a blessing to the organization that you will volunteer because in the collective mind of the organization it effectively upsets your brand image because of importance.

Start blogging to get your message out of business

Write a blog that is tailored specifically to the interests, needs, and most tough challenges of your target population. Provide fresh observations and suggestions that will highlight your expertise. Make sure that your content is easy to digest and helpful to your audience so that you become known as a problem solver.

Build a clear message and spread it

Your message needs to be consistent across all channels, to identify your values and your brand. All branding team members need to speak the same language and meet the same principles. Even simple things such as following the same graphic pattern for all advertising, blogging, or logging, if done consistently, will give your audience a sense of familiarity and make them trust your brand.

Testimonials acquire and exploit

Personal branding has allowed us to talk far too much about ourselves. As a result, we shut out the self-honored experts, gurus, and ninjas; we've become resistant to their self-promotion and "humble brags." And to truly stand out, take advantage of the "Testimonial Economy." Stop bragging about yourself – and let your clients, friends, and mentors speak for you through testimonials.

Contribute to a common cause

Through helping others, a company will immediately feel more in contact with the community's needs and make its clients feel like they're part of it for something amazing. It's also a great way to add more value as a brand and cut costs, rather than the traditional alternative.

Embrace your story and share it

You or the company's core story isn't a duplicable thing. I always advise someone who attempts to brand or rebrand to think about their story of creation and get to the soul of themselves or their product. Seek to express that in your branding then. This is you, and your company's DNA.

Benefit from your past accomplishments

Look at all of the performance that gave you success. Label them on a slip of paper. Reflect on what you've done to make those tests a success. Write down what you have done, how you have done it, who has benefited from it, and how it benefited them. Notice both examples coming from technical as well as personal experiences. Branding strategies play a vital part in every company. It's the one thing that can set the brand apart from the competition. When your branding strategies are working well, it will help the brand stand out on the market. For most businesses, the main branding item is the logo. The type of colors you select and the style depends on the nature of your company.

How to use your marketing strategy to improve your brand

"Things are manufactured in the factory but in the mind, brands are developed." -- Walter Landor, branded pioneer. The goods' intrinsic value can be easy to quantify, but the expectations of the customers are what defines the market value your brand and products have.

Of this purpose, the ability to create trust in the brand and convey that trust through your marketing to consumers is important to your company's long-term success.

Know your customer market

Business success depends for the most part on your future customers and target market. The key focus here needs to be on understanding your potent needs. You need to define what exactly your company is about and what it offers to build a brand name that people can put their faith in. A compelling argument needs to provide strong proof of a complex feedback loop.

Research is crucial here: the more you can prepare, the more you learn. Trackways in which your rivals do business, such as how they handle their clients, the price they charge, their brand, and principles in architecture, media, and other aspects. Then, use the information to understand some of the necessary customer details, such as their geographic location, shopping habits, demographics, and anything else you need to characterize them.

Enhance the best of you

To properly position your brand in front of consumers, you have to follow the four Ps: product, price, promotion, and place.

Product: Whether you are selling kitchen goods and accessories or offering luxury condos, you must have a clear vision of what your product or service is, and why it is special.

Price: The pricing choices have to consider how supply, profit margins, competition, and marketing strategies can affect the price determinations. Yet factors relating to demand elasticity will directly impact the next two Ps.

Promotion: You have to sell it in the right way if you have a product or service, and the price is determined. This includes elements such as public relations, advertisement, email marketing, social media, etc.

Place: An ideal place to display your products is essential if potential customers are to be converted into actual customers. For example, an actual transaction may not always occur online but the initial participation and conversion of a potential customer to an existing customer might take place online.

Create a Catchy Logo and tagline

To create a memorable logo you need a strong, balanced image with no small extras that clutter its look. This must fit well with the name of the organization and be in an easy-to-read font. Taglines likewise are a time-consuming operation. You have to dump the whole company in a few sentences to build a tagline, trim it down and then trim it down a little bit more. M&M's classic tagline, "Melt in your mouth, not in your hands," for instance, is catchy and reflects a straightforward message — that the hard shell prevents the chocolate from melting all over.

Select how you interact with your audience

Interaction is one of the main factors that narrow the company's divide with its target market. Once it comes to a brand voice you have to consider several things — your personality, the type of content, the sound you're going to put out, etc. You have to think of the target market and what's going to appeal to them. For example, learning how to create confidence with this group by talking with a more formal approach and no slang, if you're trying to meet senior citizens.

Render your brand ubiquitous and shiny

Brand building is an unending operation, as your target market is always going to grow rather than stabilize. Brands must be omnipresent and glossy because consumers are looking for an experience that is personalized to their needs, backed by real personal contact. Only when considering anything, a business owner can create this form of brand-from the logo to the color scheme to the tagline. A brand must build a good and consistent online presence to stand out, not seek to please everyone, deliver value, connect with other strong brands, and generate awareness about brand building.

Be your Ambassador for the Brand

Nobody knows your company better than you and your staff, and you have to be the brand ambassador of your own company and spread the word all over the world. If you connect and promote your company and brand to your customers at a more personalized level, it can help to create a more positive picture of your brand.

Promote, support, nurture

If you don't invest in promoting your brand, your target market will remain small and the results will be as well. Effective marketing of your brand can prove highly effective for your company, along with quality services and products.

Let's take a look at the best ways to market your brand:

- The power of social media these days isn't hidden from anyone. Having profiles on all major social networks, such as Facebook, Twitter, Instagram, LinkedIn, Google+ and Tumblr, etc., can help you develop your brand with a strong online presence by engaging with more personalized content.

- Attend or organize various business-related conferences, interact with your target audience and spread the word about how different you are, and the quality of the services and products you offer.

- Offer rewards such as discounts and offers with any referral to your current customers. This will help improve your customer base while providing sufficient exposure to build your brand.

Brand building can easily ensure your business reaches the right customers while boosting your sales and conversion rate. Using all of the above tips and advice, you will easily lead your business to the ultimate path to success, where your brand would be a global identifier.

The benefits of putting together a good brand

Brand value is the impression of your goods and services that consumers have, based on what they think of your brand. Apple, Google, and Microsoft are all viewed as having strong brand value.

It's hard to assign a brand a numerical value, but no matter how intangible brand equity might sound, a good brand is reaping substantial market benefits from:

- Reliability
- Remarks
- Consumer delivery

These benefits serve as tools for marketers to attract that conscientious consumer who wants to buy from a high-value brand. The conscientious consumer is willing to buy but desires value. They consider such factors in the search for value as:

Investigation. Sixty-seven percent of the purchaser's journey is completed digitally meaning the consumer's mindful desires and has a lot of information on their side about which companies they want.

Socio-evidence. It's not enough to have one great product. The attentive consumer looks to online reviews, peer recommendations, and profiles on social media for evidence of a well-liked product.

Identity and favorite. Customers are aware of a relationship between their buying decisions and their identities. They are looking to decide on a purchase that suits their brand.

All of these factors play a part in a purchase decision and all are about more than the product alone. Customers are looking at the core of their search to form a bond with a brand that they perceive as high in value.

The concept of branding

If 'brands are created in the mind,' it is important to understand how to positively advertise your business to impact the view that leads and that consumers have of your brand.

Act inside out

'The world is full of boring things-brown cows that's why so few people are paying attention,' writes Seth Godin. 'The art of building stuff worth noticing right into your product or service is outstanding marketing.' Your brand has to stand out from the herd-be a purple cow, to be regarded as important. A good brand has to do with superlatives: the best customer service, the most creative, and the happiest staff. If you want to create a strong brand, you can't limit marketing to only one department. All areas have to show consumer interest. The customer experience is the basis from which you build the rest of your marketing strategy to reinforce your mark.

Aim your message about your brand

'You have to find a community that cares deeply about what you have to say,' according to Seth Godin in his TED talk How to spread your ideas. Godin insists that creating trust requires identifying the crowd who will respect your brand and goods first, rather than just spreading a large net. It translates into: Find the communication platforms that match your target audience and *adapt your brand message to the channel of marketing*. Nike and Adidas, who are sharing a target market, each created a campaign in the 2014 World Cup. While Adidas aimed for the feeling of 'win or lose,' Nike spoke exclusively to football fans with only insiders who might understand inside jokes and follow the sport. Nike's message was stronger-more valuable-because its audience was more specific.

Use a consistent Tone of Voice

'Brand continuity' is so critical it's becoming a definite term in the marketing world. The stronger the personality of the company, the more likely they will remember you and introduce you to potential customers. Ensuring your output shares the same language, tone, and opinions eliminate any confusion, enabling your audience to form easy associations with your content. A formalized set of VoT guidelines will provide the scaffolding through which to build all potential content, aligning and blog, social post, and email to ensure you talk in one voice.

Maintain high-quality requirements

The project is to communicate visually. How you use color, shapes, font, or organize elements on a website page, email campaign, or even a product package will dictate whether your brand is perceived as valuable or not. What your package your brand will influence how it perceives and interprets your brand. A 'solid visual branding scheme' may make a small business look more effective or show the importance of a big organization. Poor architecture has a negative impact-just look at this informative spoof.

Give meaning to your marque

Beauty is in the beholder's eye the same way that beauty is considered beauty. To give its brand meaning: Make it a symbol of Status. In TED talk by Rory Sutherland, he tells the tale of a king who, to avoid drought, decreed a new crop for the potato and put guards around the fields to make the previously rejected vegetable desirable. The king had modified the idea of the importance of the crop, not the crop itself. He recommends that 'something worth defending would be worth stealing.' You may not be able to declare a 'royal crop' for your goods or company, but you should seek to build the same kind of image of your product.

Has it become symbolic? Sutherland states in the same talk that the rich in Prussia were encouraged to offer their jewelry in favor of the war effort during a battle. The pieces were replaced with cast iron replicas. Although they had decidedly less intrinsic value, the pieces came to have great symbolic value for the Prussian people because of the sacrifice they represented and became desirable during that period. Toms shoes will be a modern example. Based on the symbolic meaning of a TOMs purchase, its business model allowed them to expand into an international brand with multiple product lineages.

Link up with emotions. According to Nielsen's VP, 'emotional preference is important: while services may be identical, the emotional connection may create the impression the 'linked' brand meets the expectations of the consumer.' It means presenting a product empathetically, irrespective of its purpose. That was achieved by Google Chrome in their Dear Sophie ad. Email is a direct link. Google also used the message to communicate emotionally with customers.

Provide useful knowledge and strategic leadership in your material

Content is a prime way to express the importance of your brand and to increase its power continuously. Content can show your audience thought leadership, help build trust, as well as delight clients in becoming loyal advocates of the brand. Content adding value to your brand needs to be about quality for your audience, not quantity for your company. So, how do you base your content on adding value for the customer?

People purchase. Such semi-fictional profiles, which represent your potential clients, will contain descriptions of the preferences, complaints, pain points, and other information of your consumers to guide content development.

Stories from the buyer. Again, the consumers have to understand the interest to build brand equity. Thus, content cannot correlate with your marketing objectives. It has to be in line with the content leads and customers are searching for.

Strong words. If you intend to add value to the customer, the language you use in the conference room is not appropriate for the content. The writing in your content has to cater to the audience you are talking to.

Create Fidelity

The personalized material is the beginning of a long-term partnership. If you keep producing content that leads to interest and customers, you can keep them coming back to your brand and build loyalty.

Social media content is a way of delighting customers and getting them back into the sales funnel for future purchases. Know what channels your consumers are on and what kind of content they want to see and place reliable, tailor-made content on those channels instead.

Map marketing campaigns depending on which items consumers are interested in or are in the sales funnel. The more tailor-made and customized the content, the higher the customer's email value.

If it comes to improving a brand, consumers are the strongest allies. In a connected world where understanding defines the importance of your brand, having clients on your side will get the feedback, ratings, and social proof you need.

Strengthen your mark and further improve your marketing plan

Ultimately, brand worth comes down to distinction: the ability in the marketplace to set the brand apart. You have to be able to tell a better story and to stay successful must be consistent across all marketing platforms. Check out Type form's huge brand awareness guide to find out more about how to take a fantastic brand and get people thinking about it.

Once you have developed value from the product to the campaigns into your brand, it's important to recognize where your brand falls on the value scale and constantly change your marketing strategy to match your needs.

Everyone within the company must develop a strong brand. However, as a marketer, it is your responsibility to communicate that value to the conscious consumer who is looking for a good, high-value brand that you want to be.

Strengths and weaknesses in marketing strategy

While determining tactics, companies have to consider the impacts of external factors. A SWOT analysis is the part of a marketing strategy that analyzes your business and decides how your business can compete in the marketplace. SWOT is an acronym of strengths, weaknesses, chances, and threats. Within a marketing strategy, there are several places where the study of strengths and weaknesses is important. By understanding this approach to a marketing strategy, you can develop a comprehensive analysis of how your firm can enhance its market position.

Competitive Analysis

Part of the strengths and weaknesses that a SWOT analysis explores is how the company is performing against the competition. For determining where your strengths and weaknesses are in the marketplace, the strengths of your product offering, distribution network, and customer service levels are compared with those of the competition. This kind of analysis is critical in determining which aspects of the marketing plan need to be changed, and it also provides a way to measure success for things like customer service because it gives you something to compare your level of customer satisfaction with.

Personnel Use

Key elements in your marketing strategy are the strengths and weaknesses of how you utilize your personnel. Personnel assets include an expanded skill set, a level of personnel capable of performing tasks efficiently, and the availability of outside consultants that can enhance the capabilities of the workers. For example, because of their experience in working with international customs and performing administrative shipping tasks, you choose your shipping partners which your staff can not perform.

Weaknesses in staff utilization include a shortage of trained workers in key roles and inadequate staff utilization. For example, you may have a fully staffed warehouse for shipping products but due to production delays, you lack enough products to ship.

Headquarters

In a marketing strategy that tries to move the product towards the end-user, location can either be a strength or a weakness. Placing your distribution network along the same routes as your main shipping carrier will provide a logistical advantage in the timely delivery and reception of the product. If you need to build transportation networks just to get the product from and to a key distribution point, then you won't be able to sell the product as quickly as your competition.

Financial power

The attainment of a broad target audience with a marketing strategy requires both money and personnel resources. In simple terms, financial resources depending on the amount available can be a strength or a weakness. If your company's financial resources are small, it can commit to a marketing campaign, otherwise, some aspects of your plan will suffer. Adequate financial resources are an asset that enables you to be more competitive in the marketplace.

CHAPTER 12:

Using social media as a way to promote your Etsy store and generate customers.

The use of social media to market anything now cannot be overemphasized. I would like us to take a quick tour into understanding the concept of Social Media and to also see the reason behind the whole hype.

Social media are interactive computer-mediated technologies that facilitate information, ideas, career interests, and other forms of expression through virtual communities and networks to be created or shared. The variety of currently available, stand-alone, and integrated social media services introduces definition challenges. Users typically access social media services through web-based apps on desktops and laptops or download services that provide their mobile devices with social media functionality (e.g., smartphones and tablets). When users connect with these electronic services, they create highly interactive forums through which individuals, groups, and organizations can share, co-develop, discuss, contribute, and change online posted content that is created by users or self-curated. Networks formed via social media change the way people's groups interact and communicate or stand with the votes. This platform also refers to how people interact in virtual communities and networks, where they create, share, and/or exchange information and ideas. The Communications and Advertising Department handles the primary pages on Facebook, Twitter, Instagram, Snapchat, YouTube, and Vimeo.

- Social networking is about communication, culture, public interaction, and relationship building. It is not just a broadcast channel, or a marketing and sales tool.
- It is key to authenticity, honesty, and open dialogue.
- Social media not only lets you hear what people are saying about you but also allows you to respond. Hear first, and speak second.
- Be articulate, helpful, important, and engaging. Don't fear trying new things, just think about your efforts before you kick them off.

It refers basically to websites and applications designed to allow people to share content easily, securely, and in real-time. Although many people use mobile apps to access social media, this networking tool originated with computers, and social media can refer to any internet communication tool that enables users to exchange information widely and connect with the public. This is any digital tool that allows users to create and share content with the public quickly. The social media contains a wide array of blogs and applications. Some, such as Twitter, are skilled in exchanging links and short written posts. Others, such as Instagram and TikTok, are designed to automate picture sharing and video sharing. What is unique about social media is that it is both broad and relatively uncensored. Although certain social media sites place such restrictions — such as taking down photos that show violence or nudity — there are far fewer limits on what anyone may share with other mass media such as newspapers, radio stations, and television outlets than there.

Now before we go into the "HOW" of this section, let us look at the "WHY" we as a guide can never be too sure to assume that you know how the whole system works. So, let us dive into the "WHYs" of Social Media.

Your clients find themselves on social media.

One of the main reasons for selling your small business via social media is that your consumers invest time on those networks. Statistically, 70 percent of the U.S. population has at least one profile on social media. And the number of social media users worldwide is projected to hit about 3.1 billion people by 2021. This presents a great opportunity for small businesses that want to reach their online audience, with so many consumers using social media every day. Not only are your consumers on social media, but there is a fair chance that others will check these pages regularly. It would be easy to communicate with your target market if you are involved in the channels, they use the most frequently. In other words, don't have your audience here – go to your house! When you're not even on social media, you may miss out on a significant opportunity to communicate with your customers and take on new leads.

While marketing over social media, users would be more open to your posts.

Users are active on social media sites as these networks provide a fun and convenient way to network, keep in contact with friends and family, and stay updated to what's happening around the world. Users are not necessarily on such platforms with the understanding they would be sold to. Yet that doesn't mean social media users don't adopt their favorite brands and connect with them. Indeed, according to Marketing Sherpa, 95 percent of online adults between the ages of 18 and 34 are likely to adopt a social media brand. As people follow brands and connect with their social media accounts, however, it is because they find the material and knowledge useful in such social media campaigns. If they're looking for discounts, enjoying fun content, or just trying to know more about the brand, social media consumers are open to social media platforms engaging with brands. The explanation of why customers may be more open to your social media brand message is that social media allows you to be more conversational and show off a different side of your brand. The content you share on these platforms adds to your brand identity and lets you display your brand voice. Through social media, instead of only sending direct marketing posts, you can make genuine links with your leads and clients. It is usually something about which customers are more sensitive. Perhaps it's not uncommon for you to see on Twitter consumers and businesses debating a problem/complaint about their brand. Or maybe you've fallen at the Q & As on Instagram stories of some brands. Many advertisers see these social media platforms as a more intimate way of getting to know their followers better. And you too should.

Social media marketing can help to increase brand awareness.

The advantage of social media marketing is that it helps you increase exposure, thus increasing the brand's awareness. Your company social media accounts give new ways to share your content and to show the voice and personality of your brand. By sharing engaging content that brings value to your target market, you make your brand more available to new members and existing customers as well as more familiar. Let's say, for instance, that a new lead on social media stumbles upon your brand. They may not have heard of your business before but they can learn more about your brand and the value you offer through your social media posts. To your current customers, this same situation can apply. After seeing your social media posts on multiple networks, potential customers may be able to get to know your company better, which may boost their interest in a repeat purchase.

Social media marketing boosts inbound traffic

Your social media accounts offer your website yet another way to get more inbound traffic. That makes social media marketing an excellent tactic to complement your efforts to automate your search engine. Another way to attract new users to your site is any piece of content that you share on your social media profiles. When the visitor arrives at your site, you'll have the chance to convert. It's important to regularly publish content that connects and adds value to your target audience to get the most inbound traffic possible. The more quality content you share on your social media sites, the greater the chances you have to take in new leads and guide them back to your website. If the website is designed for sales then it's only a matter of time before these new leads are turned into customers.

Different types of social media help you meet different target audiences

Another benefit of social media marketing is that you can target various audiences strategically, depending on the platforms on which your brand is involved. You can hit your target audience and work to bring more eligible leads back to your platform, instead of just throwing your marketing message out there for all to see. Build a consistent list of demographic values for your audience-the more comprehensive, the better. The list can include their gender, age, place, interests, following brands, hobbies, etc. Understanding these principles will give you more perspective on which medium of social media you can use to achieve them. It will also help you develop content that will reach your audience and thus increasing your chances of conversion. The more relevant this traffic is, the greater your likelihood of boosting conversion rates. Whichever you seek to meet, you will find your audience on one of the many common social media networks customers use every day. The trick to getting the most out of your social media marketing is carefully choosing which platforms you want to invest in. Not sure which canals of social media are right for you?

Advertising on social media lets you target and re-target ideal customers

While social media advertisement needs a bit of an upfront cost, social ads can do a lot to supplement the organic campaigns you run on your social media platforms. Social networking networks such as Facebook help you target your ideal customers with sophisticated targeting capabilities, which allow you to drive more significant traffic to your site. This is the perfect way to make the most of your marketing outlay. With Facebook ads, you can describe your ideal customer through the advertising platform to find new potential leads. Then, Facebook allows you to deliver your ad content to those that display the same behavioral characteristics as your target audience. You will boost results when you push more important traffic to your brand site, no matter what your ad goals might be.

Social media marketing is cost-effective

One of the biggest benefits of social media marketing is that it lets you cut back on marketing expenses without sacrificing efficiency. Many of the success on social media will come from spending time in producing and publishing content, as well as talking to the fans and followers. The good news is that only a few hours a week will deliver positive results. In reality, HubSpot estimates that with as little as six hours expended on social media each week, 84 percent of marketers was able to produce increased traffic. But if you want to make social media ads a big part of your social media strategy, you will always find it cost-effective to target social media. Depending on your goals and the reach of your campaign, running paid advertisements on social media platforms such as Facebook and Twitter are fairly inexpensive. No matter how low the budget is, to meet and transform new leads, you can still make an impact on those networks.

Marketing on social media will help boost search engine rankings

You're still concentrating on enhancing the search engine optimization, there's a fair chance. But did you know search engines can use your participation in social media as a factor in their rankings? Successful brands prefer to have a healthy presence on social media, and a strong presence on social media will act as a signal to search engines that your brand is important, trustworthy, and trusted. While the ranking criteria are constantly evolving, it's a safe bet that successful social media networks will eventually benefit you. Search engines pay attention to your actions on social media, in particular connections to shared content and social signals such as likes and shares. Not only will your social media presence affect your search engine rankings, but it's important to remember that when users are searching for your brand, your social media profiles would most likely show up on Google's first list. When the user clicks on your social profiles and finds them outdated or uncommitted, they may decide to take their business to another location. That's why it's crucial not only to regularly post compelling content on your social media sites but also to periodically review your profile details and make adjustments and updates as appropriate.

Now let us proceed further to discuss the sub-topics in this section.

SOCIAL MEDIA OPTIMIZATION

Social media optimization (SMO) is the use of a variety of channels and groups to create content to raise product, service brand, or event awareness. Involved social media types include RSS feeds, social news, and bookmarking sites, as well as social networking sites such as Facebook, Instagram, Twitter, websites for video sharing and blogging. SMO is similar to search engine optimization in that web traffic generation and website visibility is the target. Generally, the optimization of social media refers to enhancing a website and its content to enable more people to use and exchange links to the website via social media and networking sites. SMO also applies to automated tools that automate this process or website experts who conduct this process on behalf of clients. SMO aims to strategically create interesting online content, ranging from well-written text to eye-catching visual photographs or video clips that inspire and entice people to connect with a website and then share it with their social media contacts and friends via its web connection. Specific examples of social media involvement include "posting and commenting, retweeting, embedding, linking, and content promotion." Social media optimization is also an efficient way to incorporate online reputation management (ORM), ensuring that an SMO approach will ensure that the negative feedback is not the first link to appear in a search engine results list if anyone publishes poor reviews of a company. Social media optimization (SMO) is the method of leveraging a variety of social media channels and communities to create viral ads to raise awareness of a product, brand, or event. Using RSS feeds, social news and bookmarking apps, as well as social networking platforms and video and blogging sites, social networking optimization requires. SMO is similar to SEO (search engine optimization) in that driving traffic to your source is the target.

Further description, Social Media Optimization (SMO) is the use of social media networks to control and expand the message and online presence of a company. Social media optimization can be used as a digital marketing tool to raise awareness of new goods and services, communicate with consumers, and boost possible negative news.

Social media optimization (SMO) is the use of social media networks to monitor and expand the message and web presence of a company.

Social media optimization can be used as a digital marketing tool to raise awareness of new goods and services, communicate with consumers, and boost possible negative news. Digital marketing can be found on various social media sites, including Facebook, Twitter, Instagram, Snapchat, YouTube, and Pinterest.

Search engine optimization (SEO) has been the norm for digital marketing initiatives for many years. Whereas social media optimization and search engine optimization have similar goals – to generate web traffic and increase awareness of a company's website – search engine optimization is the process of increasing the quality and quantity of website traffic by raising the visibility of a website or a web page for users of a web search engine, especially Google. More recently, social media marketing has come to the fore, often converging with SEO and in some cases replacing it as the most successful way to reinforce a brand, lead generation, increase the visibility of a business in the online space, and communicate with an audience. Digital marketing can be found on various social media sites, including Facebook, Twitter, Instagram, Snapchat, YouTube, and Pinterest. Social media management also guides the public to the company's web site from these social media sites, where more information can be received. For example, a campaign to raise awareness on social media about a new automobile that guides the visitor to a company website that provides information on where local dealerships are located and how to schedule a test drive.

Simple Social Media Optimization Techniques

Companies that use multiple social media platforms that use Internet-based tools designed to enhance organization and content delivery. Such tools enable an employee who is charged with creating social media content to simultaneously schedule content across multiple channels, as well as respond to any posting commitments including feedback or messages from the public. Sharing tools on social media sites allow users to almost instantly exchange content over the Internet. Despite this, many companies are seeking to build content that users pass on to their friends and contacts. This strategy, called viral marketing, seeks to reach a wider reach by getting engaged users on social media platforms to share content, rather than relying on users to find the content themselves.

Social Networking Optimization Example

Messages on social media platforms can be customized to have a stronger impact on specific individual groups. Marketers who use social media can tailor their content to demographic and geographic profiles. For example, a soft drink maker may post a message to Internet users in hot climates about how cold a beverage is. They could tell users in cold climates that drinking their beverage will remind them of summer for their audience.

Now to further give ourselves a good foundational understanding and comprehension of the power of social media. Its true power lies in influence. Facebook offers businesses with an opportunity not only to connect with consumers but also to impact them with the right information to help them make a decision. Social media gives you an incredibly powerful, inexpensive, and successful way to build your confidence — provided, of course, you're a good egg to start with.

I will now proceed to expose you to the term called;

SOCIAL MEDIA MARKETING (SMM).

Social media marketing (SMM) is the use of social media websites and social networks to market the products and services provided by a company. Social media marketing offers marketers a way to attract potential consumers, engage with current customers, and encourage the community, purpose, or tone they want. Social media marketing, also known as "digital marketing" and "e-marketing," has purpose-built data analytics tools that allow marketers to track how successful their efforts are. Websites on social media allow marketers to use a wide range of tactics and strategies to promote content and involve people. Many social networks enable users to provide detailed geographic, demographic, and personal information allowing marketers to tailor their messages to what is most likely to resonate with users. Because Internet audiences can be segmented better than more traditional marketing channels, businesses can make sure they focus their resources on the audience they want to target. Social media marketing strategies have the advantage of potentially reaching a large audience. For example, a campaign may be appealing to current and prospective clients, staff, bloggers, the media, the general public, and other stakeholders (such as reviewers from third parties or trade groups). Some of the metrics used to measure a social media marketing campaign's effectiveness include website reports (such as Google Analytics), return-on-investment (by linking marketing to sales activity), customer response rates (how much customers post about a business), and reach (how many customers share content).

Strategy for social media marketing

A major strategy used in social media marketing is to develop messages and content that will be shared between individual users and their families, friends, and coworkers. This strategy is based on word of mouth and offers many advantages. First, it increases the reach of the message to networks and users that another way a social media manager might not have been able to access. Second, when sent by someone who the recipient knows and trusts, shared content carries an implicit endorsement. Social networking strategy involves producing content that is "sticky," meaning it will get the attention of a consumer and increase the likelihood that he or she will take the desired action, such as buying a product or sharing the content with others. Marketers create viral content that is designed to quickly spread among users. Customers should also be allowed to produce and post their content, such as product reviews or feedback (known as "paid media"). Although social media marketing can bring advantages, it can also pose hurdles that businesses would not have needed to overcome otherwise. For example, the company must answer a viral video alleging that the product of a business causes people to become ill, regardless of whether the argument is valid or incorrect. Even if a firm can set the message straight, in the future consumers may be less likely to buy from the company.

ETSY AND THE MEDIA

As far as e-commerce stores are concerned, Etsy is the cornerstone for designers, producers, fashionistas, and independent organizations to make bigger and larger sales. For the off chance, you get to see your shop; to support your Etsy account with Etsy social media marketing strategies, you have to find better-promotion methodologies. There are also bunches on display that will help you broaden your permeability and social media likes. Start planning and engaging in these events by posting lovingly and commenting on various groups of people. Ensure that your posts are certified and relevant to what is under review. This data reveals that social media offers and reaches a vast crowd. When clients and online proximity need to be impacted, web-based life is the best direction to take. Social media marketing is the simplest and most economical way to showcase your creations to a large crowd of people at the same time.

There are many owners of Etsy Shop out there who see social media as "free advertisement" for their brand, just as other small businesses do. They're wasting enormous amounts of time and money on this because they know everybody is on social media because it doesn't cost them anything. Okay, the first part of that sentence is true, everybody's on social these days. But not the last part; it is far from free advertisement. You need to use the same marketing toolbox that you will use on any other marketing initiative – designing consumer profiles, targeting, segmentation, brand guidance, and, most importantly, developing relationships – to do socially well and in a way that will drive traffic and sales. And how are you going about it then?

Don't advertise yourself and the shop

It is called social media for a reason. Nothing more than just advertisement websites, and social posts. Alternatively, 70/20/10 is a reasonable strategy, 70 percent of posts share content from other users, 20 percent share their original content (useful to fans, not selling stuff!), and the final 10 percent is for promotional posts such as items, promotions, and events only.

Don't use Sellers hashtags

The number 1 mistake I see being made on sites like Twitter and Pinterest by Etsy shop owners is that they have all those useless hashtags like #etsyshop #etsyfinds #etsyhandmade #etsygifts etc. Those are hashtags which vendors use, not customers. Instead you will use hashtags which will be used by your customers to identify your products.

Get the customers comfortable

This is the number one advice I will give you. Social networking is all about sharing and engagement. Imagine if you saw a street corner marketer shouting about the latest craftsmanship they've made. Would you like to go over and buy this? Most probably not. It is the equivalent to what most social-minded Etsy shop owners are doing. Now imagine the same man but he didn't want to sell you anything at the corner of the street but wanted to meet you. Perhaps you are going out for a few days to have a coffee or lunch. Finally, the person says he sells Product X. The reaction would be very different now!

Keep a strategy

You just don't want to be willy-nilly posting it. Are you tying your posting to pattern or holiday activities? A good example of this is the sale during Thanksgiving of the Christmas items, but not during Spring Easter. Come up with ads where you offer offers to other customers or for a limited time span.

CHAPTER 13:

Facebook, Instagram, Pinterest.

Now that you have an understanding of the potentials of social media, your question might be "How do I use any of these" well, that is exactly what this section is for. We will now learn how to use some of these specific platforms to promote your shop and push things through to make sure that you get the sales you desire.

ETSY AND FACEBOOK

Given that people from many different generations are using Facebook regularly, the site is a perfect place to meet potential clients. Below are some tips for using the world's biggest social media platform. Facebook is a perfect platform to support your Etsy Shop. Honestly, it's nice to encourage just about everything. When you are using it right, it will carry you a decent chunk of traffic. Which is the reason you are right here? Great to do it. Here, by taking a look at your Facebook page insights, you can understand how to check out those Etsy BUYERS, get to know your business. It breaks down anything for you and you won't have any trouble finding it out! Additionally, enter groups specific to your shop or products. Being active is one of the essential parts of networking. Start conversations, post genuine comments that last for at least ten words! Post with some worth of details. Users would like your posts in the forums, and will eventually show up to your party or profile on Facebook. This is how you can find the true love you are looking for! Don't forget to add a few hashtags to your posts too, but not too many. They say there's 3 to a decent number of hashtags per tweet. And make sure you don't overdo it! This will help you find out the same way you do on Etsy, Pinterest, or Instagram by searching on Facebook.

Now let us see the "HOWs"

Set up a business page on Facebook

Even if you already have a personal Facebook account to represent your Etsy store, you can set up a dedicated business page. It gives you access to analytics tools from Facebook, which looks more professional. Don't forget to put a link to your Etsy shop on your Facebook business page (and add a link to your Etsy shop's Facebook page!).

Spice up your listings

When you post a Facebook page, readers can click your products directly through. This is one of the simplest and most straightforward ways for your company to exploit Facebook. Be sure to include useful information about the items in your submissions (thinking products, gifting opportunities, or other useful facts) when promoting a new item, this helps prevent your posts from becoming too promotional. Be sure to include clear calls for action in your posts such as "visit my shop to see more" or "click to buy" this offers clear action items for those reading your content and can increase clicking through.

Nurture your followings

As well as connecting from your shop to your Facebook page, consider drawing attention to it in an email to customers after they make a purchase or on your business cards and other branded materials. Give your fans a reason to follow your page, be it the exclusive first look at your new products, the content behind the scenes, or the exclusive coupon codes.

Mix things and create varieties

Vary what sort of content you share. Try to follow the rule of third parties: commit a third of your content to market new products and shop announcements; a third to business-related topics; and a third to sharing bonus things that your fans may find useful, such as DIY projects or decorating tips.

Experiment with formats and templates

Another way to mix your posts is by formatting. From posts in the carousel (posting multiple images), processing photo galleries, and video (especially live video). Consider sharing your updates through special live video announcements, which allow your followers to ask questions and engage with you directly. Pro tip: The timeline gives priority to video content, and more specifically live video on Facebook (meaning more people can see it).

Have a conversation

The great thing about all social media, particularly Facebook, is the ability to have meaningful conversations with your customers. Consider topics when thinking about ideas about content that will help you to connect with your followers. Think about answering open-ended questions and answering for ideas that can help create fruitful discussions.

Comply with your plan-and your brand

Aiming for a daily pace when posting is a good goal: 1-2 posts a day. Although it is ideal to post multiple times a day, it is better to post just once or twice a week than to post in a row for several days, and then stop. Consistency is also critical as regards brand imagery. Make sure that what you share makes sense within the context of your overall brand when posting on any social media.

Keep it open and professional

Since you will probably manage your business page via your personal Facebook account, confusing the two can be easy. Double-check that you are not posting from your account until posting to your business page (and vice-versa). Your web-page operation should represent the voice and priorities of your brand for your company.

Consider investing in Advertising on Facebook

You can use the paid ad service from Facebook either by creating a new Facebook ad or by boosting an existing post. Both options allow you to target your promotions against specific user groups based on location, interests, demographics, and more. If you're curious about paid ads but are not sure how they're going to work for your company, start with a little budget. You can launch an ad campaign directly from your Shop Manager on Facebook.

Be succinct

While Facebook offers more word count than some other social networking sites, making your posts short and sweet is still the best way to. Most users on mobile devices will read your messages, where they can have to press to see more of the text. Keep the captions minimal (one to three sentences), especially if you want readers to click on a link.

Track your results

Through building a business page on Facebook, you gain access to the Insights, the analytics tools on Facebook. Look at a variety of metrics, including comments, likes, and views, to get a sense of overall interaction with followers.

Using your Facebook profile as a business platform

Business pages on Facebook give you more space to share tons of details about your company. If you're running a multifaceted company that involves a website, blog, and Etsy store, your company page on Facebook can be a great place to tie it all together. You can keep shoppers in the loop there on something new that happens with your company.

INSTAGRAM AND ETSY

Use Instagram to share your visual brand's resources, processes, and products is a simple way to show what makes your company special and communicate with followers. This famous photo-sharing app promotes spontaneity and provides an alternative to copy-heavy marketing – you can create brand awareness through visual storytelling. Etsy is by far the best eCommerce platform for innovative entrepreneurs, and with good reason: it is a great site that enables craftsmen and artists to link to their audience with a few clicks of their mouse to sell their handcrafted works and handmade products. Anyone with an Etsy account will also have access to a range of fantastic tools for marketing, analytics, and advertisement. These resources provide you with a great arsenal that you can use to drive traffic to your shop and turn your passion project into revenue and sales. Etsy is certainly a forum for you whether you are a marketing novice or a business savvy professional. Instagram is by far one of the best ways to generate true, high-quality leads for your digital business because of the individuals, goods, and interests that most often pertain to Etsy unique site. Suffice it to say that I think there are far quicker approaches for steady and growing sales on Etsy than setting up a follow-up social network, such as mastering marketing off Etsy and knowing search engine optimization. So how do you create and develop the loyal followership and community of loving people who fall all over to buy everything you put out?

Know when your customers are online

The only way to do this is to set up a business profile that I would strongly recommend you do. Once you have built a business profile, you will have access to loads of stats about location, age, gender, and the most famous times your followers are online. You can use this information to post to your specific audience at the best times, which will depend on a lot of factors such as who you sell to, where they are located, and the circumstances of their lives (working vs. staying at home moms, college students vs. ages 60s and up, etc.)

Comment on articles by others

Social media, well, they are social. For every comment, you don't have to write a paragraph, but even easy comments like "It's cute! What a cute living/baby/dog room!" Show commitment, and encourage people to click on your profile. But a word of caution — do not just comment with an emoji or a super-general comment like "That's awesome 'There are bots' people can pay for that will comment on the profiles of other people for you, and these kinds of comments are very typical of these bots. It also makes it look like you're going through and spamming people on every post you come across with the same emoji (which might be true ...) and doesn't inspire them to want to connect with you.

Hashtags

Hashtags are key to finding themselves on Instagram. This should probably be the number one tip of advice, because you will never find yourself in the millions upon millions of Instagram users without hashtags, particularly as a new user or new account that promotes your Etsy shop. I think it is particularly important to use hashtags for creative entrepreneurs who are trying to show off their creations/products, and it is a good idea to research common hashtags in your particular area of work. I built the Ultimate List of Etsy hashtags that you can copy to your posts and add to them. These include both Etsy-specific hashtags and hashtags which are common for handmade items. I would also recommend tossing the product you are mentioning into certain specific hashtags, the product category it is, the season it applies to, the team it matches, your venue, etc.

Stories on Instagram

These days, Instagram stories are HUGE. Again, you don't need to reinvent the wheel here, nor do you need to let people access your personal life behind the scenes. Nevertheless, looking at your company, the creation process, a new product line, or your office behind the scenes, you as an individual and your business will attract interest. You can also use the polls and answer boxes to ask your audience questions, ask them their views about new products, or vote on their favorite of a few options. There's a lot of better organic traffic and feedback on stories in my experience, so the more you use it the better. It also allows people to become familiar with you as the face behind the brand — you don't have to look perfectly composed or finished. Just be yourself on video and your enthusiasm for your products and energy will show through in your company.

Marketing influencer

Over the past several years influencer marketing has grown into a huge industry. Connecting with influencers with a target market close to you can be a wonderful way to team up for promotion. Often you can find amazing influencers that will only advertise your goods for the cost of the product (no extra compensation) and provide you with beautiful pictures to use as well. One word of advice-tons of accounts are out there promising to promote your product for a fee. Don't fall into that trap. Such accounts have often bought followers (these are fake accounts purchased to inflate their number of followers) and so the interaction on the accounts is often either low or non-existent. If you see an account with numbers like 60,000 followers on each photo and 30 likes, you know the followers are not legitimate. The likelihood that your promotion will pay off in any way is extremely low. Another word of warning-once you get established selling on Etsy and start getting a decent social media following, you will be asked to donate your goods several times so that people can "review" them on their blog / YouTube / social media. You must research the institutions that those people run before deciding whether to do it or not. Just because somebody wants to work with you (i.e. get your products for free) doesn't mean it's good for you at all. Make sure your company profits from this before you commit to anything like that.

Consistency

Instagram's golden rule (and all social media): You need to be consistent. Whether that means batching your work and spreading it out, or setting up a time and posting every day at the same time, you have to communicate with your followers regularly or the interest will die off. Instagram's algorithm relies on users interacting with your feed, so if you're going for days or weeks without posting something, it tells Instagram that no one is interested in your stuff (because no one is interacting because there's nothing new to connect with) and then it dramatically reduces the interaction even after you start posting. The only way to continuously increase your reach is by regularly sharing great content — content that your followers are interested in, that they want to connect with, and that keeps building up your following. Instagram can be a great way to promote your business, interact with clients, build a community, and give your brand a face and voice. It's my favorite way of free promotion by far and can help drive traffic to your Etsy shop as you build it bigger and bigger and connect more with the people that follow you. Being consistent with your Instagram - a consistent brand identity, consistent picture style, voice, and frequency of posting is critical to making people a member of a community you're creating for your loyal fans.

ETSY AND PINTEREST

Pinterest is fun, easy to use, and I will admit a little addictive, as any regular pinner would tell you. Every day, millions of people use Pinterest to discover their interests, find items (like yours) to purchase and interact with people who have similar interests. The more people pin, discover, and expose their goods, the more likely it will be for new customers to discover their business. Using those tips to join the pinning group and promote your Pinterest brand.

Open a Business page for Pinterest. Etsy vendors are usually musicians, dealers, and artisans. So, it may be that they think more of themselves as individuals than as enterprises. Nevertheless, sellers at Etsy need to open business accounts on Pinterest. There are other benefits of getting a Pinterest business page, such as promoting your business name, as Huff points out in his book, and it is a prerequisite of the terms and conditions of Pinterest.

Be a member of the Family. Pinterest is a group, like other social media networks. It is necessary, when a seller markets in that culture, not only to promote goods and ask for publicity but to contribute genuinely. Do not only add your things with that in mind. Start a lot of Pinboards and post things that suit your brand. When you're selling baby clothes, posting pins about mothering, child care, schooling, and nursery furniture will be compatible with the goods and industry of your Etsy shop. If you're selling hand-tied fishing flies, posting river and fish images or fly rod pictures may be a good strategy.

Build a variety of boards that highlight the personality and taste of your store, and ensure that each board has enough pins to make it look meaningful so pinners can look like it's worth following. Give simple names to the pages, so that people can easily grasp what's on them. But don't think about being creative — just limit names to 20 characters or less so they don't get truncated. Categorize each board and provide a summary, as this will encourage individuals to follow your boards and help you appear in searches.

Don't be afraid. Being a successful pinner, yourself is a great way to get people pinning their things. Follow boards of other people, then tag and comment on pins that inspire your shop and relate to them. This will help customers get a sense of what is different about your store. What type of stuff are you meant to tag/expose and how? What do you have to say about comments? A strong thumb rule: Just be yourself. So, don't forget to let your clients know that you're at Pinterest. For example, when you exchange messages with them include a link to your Pinterest profile to allow them to follow you and expose your pins.

Pin like a professional. Seek to pin your followers at least once a day so they get fresh material in their home feeds. Also, you may want to pin all day instead of all at once. And don't feel like you just need to pin your things. You can say a much richer story about who you are, what your shop stands for, and what you are inspired by getting pins from other people. Pinning can also be used as a way to tell stories about your goods. Pinning a handful of pins that tell a fuller story together will catch the imagination and help you develop a deeper link with pinners. A shop that sells women's coats, for example, might pin a product picture alongside pins of beautiful winter scenery to help inspire pinners about the magic they can experience outdoors in the wintertime. However, note that most people will see the pins individually when they find and tag the pins they like best.

Understand that Pinterest is a platform for visuals. The customers connect with the pictures, so you'll need to make sure you've got good product photography for your Etsy products. For your Pinterest pins, you'll want more than just product pictures on a white backdrop, which is a best practice on Etsy. To make your product visually appealing, consider lifestyle photos, close-ups, or even picture filters.

CHAPTER 14:

Scaling up, going pro, and growing your Etsy Empire.

Etsy is way more than just a marketplace. I see it as an alternative to global mass production and consumption, and a protest against the branding of corporations. It's their vote for authenticity and good old craftsmanship, and an ethical alternative to big companies buying. And it has helped fuel a larger articles market, from bedsheets to beef jerky, pretending to be a homespun, craft, or otherwise handmade. Etsy, in effect, has ballooned and benefited from a growing market for such shopping, currently offering over 29 million listings of handmade jewelry, pottery, sweaters, etc. At the end of last year, it had 54 million users, of which 1.4 million listed an item for sale and nearly 20 million made at least one purchase in 2014, according to its IPO prospectus.

Now coming down to you as a seller, how do you measure and scale up, how do you keep up? As I said, consistency is key, then how do you manage to keep this up. It is time to sit down and draw up a list of what slows you down. What will stop you from placing 50 orders tomorrow, and how you can scale up your Etsy Company to keep up.

Time (does it take too long to build orders?)

This may be the symptom of a specific problem. Using the equipment? Was it able to answer a great many orders? If not, then an upgrade is necessary. OR maybe you're making every aspect of your item yourself. If it takes too long you put a limit on your business which prevents you from scaling up your Etsy shop. It's a horrible responsibility when the shop depends on you 100 percent. See if you can order pieces of your item pre-made, or hire people to help. Better yet: Is there a piece of equipment to relieve your burden? Do some homework, and still hire machines in front of people.

Cash (I cannot afford the deliveries)

The cost of your supplies will be factored to the item's final price. Your supply expense will be returned +15%(minimum). And if your item goes viral, the simple fact it sells means you can afford the supply. Seek to find a wholesaler that you can rely on for well-priced supplies FAST if you're planning for sales that haven't come yet (like at Christmas) Note that supplies are an investment in your company and a source for the future. They are non-negotiable and if you fail to afford them you will need to reassess your pricing.

It is too difficult (to make a lot of that item)

This will put a headline on your business. This might not be the best option if your item is time-consuming or difficult to make. Seek to differentiate from item to item. 90 percent of your shop should be simple, easy and 10 percent (or less) more complicated custom-made pieces. If you're losing out on how to do this, consider digital downloads. Can you sketch patterns? Tutorials on this? Printable slideshows? What happens to a kit? Can you send your customer the supplies they need to make their version of your products by hand?

CHAPTER 15:

Why most shops fail, and how to avoid that.

Major reasons why shops fail on Etsy are not farfetched. I will highlight some of them and then we will look into how to avoid these failure-steps together.

- Wrong product choice
- Wrong category choice
- Ugly Pictures
- Poor Packaging and Shipping
- Lack of networking
- Insufficient Inventory
- Incomplete Description
- Inadequate marketing and SEO
- High/Low Pricing
- Bad customer service

Now that we have seen reasons that you are all familiar with already, let us see how we can avoid these mistakes, to ensure that our shops stay flourishing for as long as we want.

Many vendors make the mistake of concentrating on goods that are never going to sell. It is a waste of energy and can cause anger and eventually can you to give up. By conducting research before determine which products to sell, you will prevent this issue. Research shops that sell similar products to yours. You want to check for common products, upward trends, and things that sell well. In short, you want high-demand and low-cost products.

Similar to selecting the wrong items to sell, selecting an undesirable or crowded category will make sales challenging or almost impossible for you to obtain. By conducting research before determining which products to sell, you will prevent this error. Search for high-demand segments and low-offer. The best profits are always found in unique niches in every industry.

Most sellers make the mistake of using blurred, fuzzy, or hideous images on their shop accounts. This can scare off potential buyers because they too cannot see what they are buying. Admittedly, this is one region in which I have failed. To make your shop look professional you do not need to be an expert photographer. Seek to take pictures of the product with the best lighting possible. Some shop owners end up employing an accomplished photographer. It is one aspect where I disagreed with the sellers I met. Some were adamant that the pictures in this list would be better. I ended up leaving it in this role because I was very shocked to find that some of my early selling products didn't have flawless pictures. Do not make the same error that I made; I am sure that my profits could have been even higher!

Errors in packaging can result in broken items and orders which never reach their destination. Errors in shipping can quickly eat into your earnings and place you at a competitive disadvantage. Shipping can be difficult, and the price differences are large. How difficult shipping and packing can be was one of the key issues I overlooked when opening my store. I didn't even really think about it until I got my first shipment, and I didn't even have a box that would suit the product. I promised myself after this first sale that I would never let that happen again. Before selling any product, have all of your packaging materials picked. Please ensure materials are included to protect your delicate goods. Take the time to study the different shipping companies and see which one is offering the best price for the requirements of your item. Save time and money at home by printing out your shipping labels. Most shipping companies offer their customers free packaging supplies, depending on the options that you choose. Write letters of thanks by hand for every sale!

One of the main reasons why Etsy shops struggle is because of a lack of networking. Lack of networking will leave you isolated and lead to more mistakes being made and lessons being learned the hard way. Shops that network typically see good results in several areas and failure to take advantage of this tool would place you behind other stores. This is the key tool I used to raise traffic to my website and make sales explode. This is one of the main reasons I created this website too. Interact on our Facebook page or in our comments section with other sellers. Tell other helpful shop owners. Search to enter and remain involved with related Etsy teams.

Another reason Etsy stores struggle is that they don't hold enough inventory. The amount of your inventory is critical as it affects turnaround time, or the time it takes for your items to ship. The design of your pieces may take a significant amount of time because they are handmade. Unless notified otherwise, most customers will expect the non-custom items to be complete and will be ready to ship in a short time. Timing is critical since many consumers have deadlines and are purchasing your products as birthday, wedding, or vacation gifts. Customers often procrastinate and purchase without taking into account delays. Another mistake related to inventory is the failure to take proper quality control steps. It will result in the delivery of incorrect orders or faulty goods by customers. It will frustrate them, which will also save you more because of higher returns. The way to prevent issues with the inventory is to make sure you stock up the inventory as soon as possible. In particular, building up your inventory rates before the holidays or other peak demand periods is critical. When you get incredibly busy, you may need to enlist the support of family members or friends to support you. Always, make sure you keep the turnaround time listed on your site up-to-date and correct. Create quality control procedures to ensure every order is accurate, in good condition, and ready for shipment.

One of the main reasons Etsy shops struggle is that they provide incomplete or inaccurate explanations of the product listing. Shoppers come to Etsy to purchase exclusive handmade pieces they won't be able to find anywhere. The explanations are especially relevant for items purchased on Etsy since the items can't be viewed by your customers in person. They'll concentrate on the little details because they can't hold the product physically. If your item is particularly special, clients may not even be familiar with the purpose of your product. Unless you have short details, purchasing your goods would not be easy for consumers and you will not be having sales. The best way to prevent that mistake is to make sure your listing is correct, thorough, and long enough. Rather than assume that consumers understand exactly what your product is, support them by offering clear information and specifics on each item, as well as advice about what types of circumstances or occasions it would be suitable for. You will incorporate some of your personality, and ensure that you use vocabulary specific to your target clients.

Many shop owners do not offer attention and focus their merits to marketing, and Search Engine Optimization (SEO). When you neglect marketing and SEO, multiple pages deep on the search results will conceal or cover your goods. You might be able to make some sales, but it's going to be an incredibly difficult to develop. I might write an entire Etsy Marketing / SEO novel! There are plenty of free ways to sell on Etsy and at the top of Etsy (and Google) search results have your goods pop up. This involves using the names, headlines, and keywords correctly.

Another factor Etsy shops struggle to handle pricing. Faults in pricing can go either way. You can list an item too high and have no one buy your product, or you can list your product too low, leaving money to the table. Look at the prices of the rivals and see to it that yours is compatible with those in the business. Before you launch, you might want to make your prices a little lower to draw the attention and undercut the other sellers. It will potentially make the other sellers nuts, but this tactic has worked for me, and I use it all the way. It is important to remember that I was temporarily keeping my prices lower, and I was still making a good profit on my goods. It is an indication that I was not saturating the product field or group I was selling into. You can use pricing to control demand once you study the market, and are experienced.

The main reason most Etsy shops fail is due to bad customer service. Nothing was optimized when I first started my shop. I hadn't learned how to correctly avoid any of the errors I described above. Somehow, I still wonder why to this day a young lady from North Carolina ordered one of my wine racks. I made sure my first customer gets the best customer service possible and it paid off. She left me with a five-star rating and it helped to get more orders coming in. For the first deal, I didn't even end up making money but it certainly priced it. If my first client hadn't been treated with excellent customer service, she could have missed her review or even worse put down a poor review. My shop would never have had a chance. To avoid this error, make sure to reflect above all else on the experience of your client. Go beyond and beyond by delivering excellent service which will make you stand out in contrast with other shops. Be respectful & always courteous. Make sure all messages are answered promptly and accurately. Follow up after your order with your clients, and thank them again.

Printed in Great Britain
by Amazon